The Teaching Assistant's Guide to Dyslexia

Also available from Continuum

The Teaching Assistant's Guide to Dyslexia

*Gavin Reid
and Shannon Green*

continuum

Continuum International Publishing Group

The Tower Building	80 Maiden Lane
11 York Road	Suite 704
London, SE1 7NX	New York, NY 10038

www.continuumbooks.com

British Library Cataloguing-in-Publication Data
A catalogue record for this book is available from the British Library.

ISBN 0-8264-9759-4 (paperback)
   978-0-8264-9759-8 (paperback)

Library of Congress Cataloging-in-Publication data
Reid, Gavin
   The teaching assistant's guide to dyslexia / Gavin Reid and Shannon Green
      p. cm.
   Includes bibliographical references.
   ISBN-13: 978-0-8264-9759-8 (pbk.)
   ISBN-10: 0-8264-9759-4 (pbk.)
  1. Dyslexic children--Education. 2. Teachers' assistants. I. Green, Shannon. II. Title.
   LC4708.R453 2007
   371.91´44--dc22

2007028360

Typeset by Kenneth Burnley, Wirral, Cheshire
Printed and bound in Great Britain by MPG Books Ltd, Bodmin, Cornwall

Contents

Contents

This book refers to Teaching Assistants; however, we recognize that there are many different names for this important role. So this book is also for Classroom Aides, Classroom Assistants, Educational Assistants, Special Education Assistants, Learning Support Assistants, Paraeducators, Special Needs Assistants, TAs, Teacher Aides and Teacher Assistants.

Introduction

Purpose of the book

The term 'teaching assistant' is a blanket term. The range of duties and responsibilities of teaching assistants vary considerably from school to school and country to country. Some have considerable responsibility and are involved in planning and assessment as well as in the teaching and learning process. Others may have less responsibility and carry out prescribed tasks. Irrespective of the role of teaching assistants, they are in a key position to have close interaction with children and to obtain a good understanding of their needs. This book is important for that reason. Children with dyslexia have specific teaching and learning needs, and many of these require an understanding of the learning process that will in fact benefit all children. It is hoped therefore that this book will form the basis of training programmes for teaching assistants and provide guidance in their everyday role in the classroom.

How to use the book

This book could be used as a reference book for teaching assistants in any country, as the needs of children with dyslexia are the same irrespective of the country or culture. We have included in the book specific questions and some suggested activities that may assist in this training process. Essentially however this is a practical book and we have sought to cover the needs of children from the early years to final school examinations.

It is also hoped this book will be used by teachers and by school management. We have highlighted throughout the importance of teaching assistants being part of a team and this has implications for both teachers and school management. It is important that all personnel in the school recognize and appreciate the potential impact of teaching assistants in relation to the development of learning skills and learning materials.

The role of teaching assistants in supporting dyslexic students

Increasingly children with dyslexia are being included in mainstream schools. Some of these schools will have teaching assistants specifically designated for these students – others however may not, and the teaching assistant may have to deal with a range of children and a range of needs. It is important therefore that teaching assistants are familiar with dyslexia as this knowledge and understanding will be invaluable in whatever role they have in the school.

Structure and key points of the book

We have tried to make the book as user-friendly as possible. We have provided a detailed contents page and a list of key points at the beginning and the end of each chapter. The book can therefore be used as a quick source of information, as well as a more extended training manual. We have also included questions and activities throughout each chapter to prompt extended thinking and to clarify some of the points made in the chapter. We also hope the glossary at the end will be useful, particularly since some teaching assistants may find themselves in classrooms with very little previous training.

We sincerely hope the book will be useful in providing teaching assistants with knowledge and understanding of dyslexia, but above all we hope the book can be a catalyst for extended training and enhanced recognition of the status and the potential impact of teaching assistants within the school.

1

Introduction to dyslexia

This book is intended to be a source of information to promote understanding as well as an avenue for training for teaching assistants in the area of dyslexia. Throughout the book questions will be highlighted. This will help to monitor the readers' understanding of the practical impact and the potential of the points made throughout the book.

The recognition of the nature of dyslexia and the implications of the characteristics of dyslexia for teaching, preparing materials and for student learning is of paramount importance in today's inclusive classrooms and society. This is of vital importance for teaching assistants, who often have some responsibility for the day-to-day contact with dyslexic students. This book therefore is a training manual designed to provide teaching assistants with the knowledge and the confidence to interact informatively with students with dyslexia, as well as with parents and colleagues.

This first chapter will focus on:

- definitions of dyslexia and the implications of these for the teaching assistant's role
- characteristics of dyslexia
- some of the issues relating to the dyslexia debate, such as strategies for literacy teaching, the overlap with other specific difficulties and issues relating to bilingual cultures.

Defining dyslexia

It is important that teaching assistants have a sound knowledge of the key definitions of dyslexia. Some definitions can be neurological, and others theoretical. For example the definition below from the International Dyslexia Association is very sound and has considerable consensus, but it needs to be contextualized for teaching purposes.

Dyslexia is a specific learning disability that is neurological in origin. It is characterized by difficulties with accurate and/or fluent word recognition and by poor spelling and decoding abilities. These difficulties typically result from a deficit in the phonological component of language that is often unexpected in relation to other cognitive abilities and the provision of effective classroom instruction. Secondary consequences may include problems in reading comprehension and reduced reading experience that can impede growth of vocabulary and background knowledge. (Adopted by the IDA Board, November 2002 and by the National Institutes of Health, 2002 (www.idabc.com).)

For our purposes here it is more appropriate to focus on a practical or working definition of dyslexia. The one below can be adapted for this purpose:

dyslexia is a **processing difference** experienced by people of all ages, often characterized by difficulties in literacy, it can affect other **cognitive areas** such as memory, speed of processing, time management, co-ordination and directional aspects. There may be **visual and phonological difficulties** and there is usually some **discrepancy** in performances in different areas of learning. It is important that the **individual differences and learning styles** are acknowledged since these will affect outcomes of learning and assessment. It is also important to consider the **learning and work context** as the nature of the difficulties associated with dyslexia may well be more pronounced in some learning situations (Reid 2003).

The key points in this definition are outlined in bold above. The list below explains the implications of these points.

- *processing difference* – this means that how information is remembered and retained can be different in students with dyslexia. They will likely use different types of strategies and have preferences for certain types of learning, particularly visual. This can have implications for planning a lesson and for presenting information.
- *can affect cognitive areas* – this relates to memory, understanding and processing speed as well as the development of phonological processing needed for reading.
- *may be visual and phonological difficulties* – this indicates that dyslexia can relate to difficulties with sounds but there can also be visual difficulties that can also affect reading and reading fluency.
- *discrepancy in performances in different areas of learning* – this indicates that students with dyslexia can show strengths in some areas while in others they may have significant and unexpected difficulties.
- *important that individual differences and learning styles are considered* – this suggests that dyslexia is individual. You may have two or three dyslexic children in your class and they may each have different profiles and learning styles.
- *important to recognize the importance of the learning and work context* – this indicates that in some situations a persons dyslexia can be more severe than in other contexts. It is important to recognize this and to try to avoid putting dyslexic children into unsupported learning situations where they can be potentially vulnerable.

Relate this working definition to a child in your class. Show how he or she may have difficulties at each of the bullet points above. Show how you might consider dealing with these. This last point will be followed up later in the book.

A definition can provide a framework but it is also a good idea to make a list of fairly typical characteristics that may be displayed by students with dyslexia. These are shown below (see also pages 18–20).

Recognizing dyslexia: characteristics of dyslexia

Pre-school and early years

Concern may be raised if the child shows some or all of the following:

- forgetfulness
- speech difficulty
- reversal of letters
- difficulty remembering letters of the alphabet
- difficulty remembering the sequence of letters of the alphabet
- a history of dyslexia in the family
- coordination difficulties, e.g. bumping into tables and chairs
- difficulty in tasks which require fine motor skills such as tying shoelaces
- slow at reacting to some tasks
- reluctance to concentrate on a task for a reasonable period of time
- confusing words which sound similar
- reluctance to go to school

- signs of not enjoying school
- difficulty identifying and/or producing rhymes
- reluctance to read
- difficulty learning words and letters
- difficulty with phonics (sounds)
- poor memory
- losing items
- difficulty forming letters
- difficulty copying
- difficulty colouring
- poor organization of materials.

Primary school (early stages)

- hesitant at reading therefore has poor reading fluency
- poor word attack skills – difficulty decoding new words and breaking these words down into syllables
- poor knowledge of the sounds of words
- difficulty recognizing where particular sounds come in words
- spelling difficulty
- substitution of words when reading for example 'bus' for 'car'.

Primary school (later stages)

Same points as early stages, but also:

- behaviour difficulties
- frustration and inconsistencies in performances
- may show abilities in other areas of the curriculum apart from reading
- attention and concentration difficulties.

Secondary school

Same points as primary school, but also:

- takes a long time over homework
- misreads words
- relies on others to tell him or her information
- poor general knowledge
- takes longer than most others in the class on written tasks
- may not write a lot in comparison to his or her knowledge on the subject
- difficulty copying from books
- may spend a great deal of time studying with little obvious benefit
- may not finish classwork or examinations as runs out of time
- there may be a degree of unhappiness because of difficulties in school that may manifest itself in other areas.

Identify at least six of the characteristics above for the age group you are involved with. Show, with specific examples, the evidence you have that they are showing these characteristics.

The dyslexia debate

It is important to be aware of the debate about dyslexia. The debate stems from a number of different sources such as the use of the terms 'dyslexia' and 'learning disabilities', the criteria for recognition of dyslexia and the most effective teaching approaches for students with dyslexia. Some of the key issues for debate will be discussed here.

Insights into the current debate

- **Literacy teaching** – There are different approaches to the teaching of reading. Basically this involves approaches called bottom-up and top-down. Bottom-up approaches look at the details of the individual word, letter or sound and this is the starting point. Top-down approaches on the other hand focus on the whole word and language experience and the use of context. Ideally one should be seeking a balanced approach between top-down and bottom-up. A checklist for a balanced approach can be seen below:

- sight vocabulary
- differentiation of different sounds
- involvement with the narrative
- creative thinking
- visual imagery
- a meaningful context for the reader
- fluency in reading.

■ **Phonics approach** – There is strong evidence to suggest that phonological factors are of considerable importance in reading. Children with dyslexia often have decoding problems in reading because they are unable to break words down into their constituent components, and to generalize from one word to another, meaning every word they read is unique. This emphasizes the importance of teaching sounds/phonemes and ensuring that the child has an awareness of the sound/letter correspondence. This will be developed in a later chapter of this book.

■ **Language experience** – Many of the approaches for dyslexic children are bottom-up and based on an understanding of phonics. It is also important that top-down approaches to reading are implemented. These will benefit dyslexic children by promoting language experience. Language experience can be achieved through discussion and it is important that even if the child cannot access the print content of some books, the language, concepts, ideas and narrative should be discussed. This helps to make literacy motivating and emphasizes the view that literacy is more than just reading.

Select a reading programme or sets of readers you are familiar with and reflect on the elements of these that are 'bottom-up' or 'top-down'. Come to a decision as to whether the programme is a balanced one.

Provision

There is an ongoing debate into the most effective type of provision for students with dyslexia. Many argue that they benefit from one-to-one or small group tuition. Others suggest that their needs can be met in larger groups with support. As a teaching assistant you will very likely experience both situations.

Reflect on the advantages and disadvantages of both these teaching situations – one-to-one and small group tuition. How would you need to adapt your practices for each of these?

Overlap with other learning difficulties

One of the key issues in dealing with children with dyslexia in the classroom situation is the overlap between dyslexia and the other learning difficulties. There can often be some overlap between dyslexia, dyspraxia (coordination difficulties), dysgraphia (handwriting difficulties), ADHD (attention difficulties) and dyscalculia (number difficulties) (see Glossary for more extensive definitions).

The important point is that materials prepared for dyslexia

may, in some situations, be suitable for children with other difficulties. For example, many children with learning difficulties often have difficulties with working memory (see Glossary) and speed of processing. If you are working in a class with a group of children who have some of the problems above it may be useful to target the difficulty you are working with – e.g. working memory – and develop materials for that area. This would mean that children with dyspraxia, dysgraphia and ADHD may also benefit as well as the child with dyslexia. It could also be suggested that we need to look beyond the label and instead look at the learning profile.

Top Tips!

Try to identify the actual barriers to learning that are preventing the child from accessing the curriculum. To do this you need to look beyond the label.

Multilingualism and dyslexia

This is also an area of concern as it is recognized that some bilingual or multilingual students may have undiagnosed dyslexia. Often if a dual language student is experiencing difficulties in literacy the cause is attributed to bilingual factors – in fact the cause may be dyslexia. For that reason it is an issue. Additionally it is important to prepare teaching materials for dual language students that are culturally appropriate as well as being at the right reading level. This can present challenges, which are widely recognized in the literature (Cline 2000).

Make a list of the different languages and cultures in your class and then look through the reading books in the resource room and note those that are culturally appropriate for different groups. The important point to note is that these materials may still need to be differentiated for children with dyslexia.

Implications for teaching assistants

A major evaluation of the role of teaching assistants in the UK conducted by HMI (Ofsted 2002), shows that teaching assistants in primary schools have played an important part in the implementation of the national literacy and numeracy strategies by providing support to both teachers and pupils in the classroom. The report suggests that teaching assistants also played a key role in the intervention and catch up programmes such as early literacy support and additional literacy support. The report however recognizes the competing demands placed on teaching assistants. They need to provide practical support for teachers such as managing and preparing materials, but are also involved, according to the report, in the implementation of literacy and numeracy initiatives. This double role of preparing and implementing is demanding and it is crucial that support and training are available for teaching assistants to help them deal with the demands of the role.

The report actually recommends that the literacy and numeracy strategies, and other government initiatives involving teaching assistants, should be coordinated to make it easier for schools to meet the training requirements and manage the work of teaching assistants efficiently.

For teaching assistants to get the support they need the school management needs to recognize the potential workload tensions they might be experiencing. In relation to supporting students with dyslexia this can result in additional demands for teaching assistants as dyslexia itself may not be fully recognized by some schools. We have always suggested that supporting students with dyslexia is a whole-school responsibility. The teaching assistant should be a component of the whole-school responsibility.

Two key factors therefore in the role of teaching assistants are working with others and working independently.

Working with others

This is an important aspect of the role of teaching assistants and often success in this capacity relies to a great extent on the school climate and the type of school organization.

> Note the occasions in a week when you are directly working with others in the school or out with the school. Note the challenges you have experienced during that time but also note the benefits you have gained from working with others.

Working independently

Increasingly this is becoming more important for teaching assistants. The UK government guidelines suggest four levels of teaching assistants and this will be reflected in their duties and training. It can be seen that level four mentions taking responsibility for agreed learning activities under an agreed system of supervision, and this involves planning, preparing and delivering learning activities for individuals or groups.

ACTIVITY

Note the occasions when you are working independently in the course of a week. Make a special note of the support and the supervision you are experiencing.

Chapter summary

- A working, or practical, definition of dyslexia is important as it can help you understand the barriers to learning that have to be overcome.
- It is important to recognize the strengths and difficulties experienced by learners with dyslexia.
- It is also important to acknowledge the individual learning style of students with dyslexia.
- You need to be familiar with the range of characteristics that can be seen in dyslexic children and note that these can be different at different stages of their school career.
- A balanced approach to reading is necessary offering a mixture of 'bottom-up' phonics approaches and 'top-down' language experiences approaches.
- It is also important to note the overlap between dyslexia and the other learning disabilities and to recognize that planning needs to consider more than just the label, but the profile of the child.
- There are many additional challenges faced in supporting children with dyslexia and multilingualism is one that needs to be recognized. It is important to ensure that culturally appropriate materials are available.
- It is crucial that teaching assistants have the support of the school management in both the implementing of their role and in their training.

2

Identifying needs –
linking assessment with support

The role of the teaching assistant

It is unlikely that teaching assistants will be undertaking an assessment, but it is important that they know what type of difficulties children with dyslexia display, and importantly how to implement and interpret the results of an assessment. This chapter will:

- discuss the role of the teaching assistant in the gathering of information
- examine the characteristics of dyslexia and how these can be recorded
- look at the implications of test/assessment results for classroom practice
- show how observation can be used for gathering data
- clearly show how assessment can be linked to support
- describe the barriers to learning experienced by children with dyslexia
- look at different forms of classroom-based assessment.

The assessment process – data gathering

Teaching assistants should be familiar with the assessment process. This process includes the gathering of data from a wide range of sources and is not solely dependent on test data. Some of this information will come from discussions with parents and through observation in the classroom. The teaching assistant can have an important role to play in these aspects of data gathering.

It is important to note here that the degree of dyslexia experienced by a child can vary according to the context. The dyslexic difficulties will be more obvious in some learning environments and contexts, while in other environments they may not be so obvious. This means that observation can be very important as a means of gathering information on the learner, the teaching approaches and the classroom environment. If there is a lot of teacher talk, for example, dyslexic characteristics can be more obvious, while if the focus is on discussion, visual learning and creativity they may be less obvious. It is vital therefore that teaching assistants have a good awareness of the characteristics of dyslexia, especially in the early years. The research indicates that early identification is crucial for effective intervention and it is often too easy for children with dyslexia to escape detection as their difficulties can be mistaken for immaturity, general learning difficulties or developmental lag.

Characteristics of dyslexia – checklists for teaching assistants

1. Pre-school and early years checklist

Characteristic	Frequency	Examples	Support needed
Forgetfulness			
Speech difficulty			
Reversal of letters			
Difficulty remembering letters of the alphabet			

Difficulty remember-ing the sequence of letters of the alphabet			
Coordination difficulties			
Difficulties with fine motor skills			
Slow in completing tasks			
Poor concentration			
Reluctance to read			
Difficulty copying			
Difficulty forming letters			
Difficulty colouring			
Poor organization of materials			

2. Primary school checklist

Characteristic	Frequency	Examples	Support needed
Poor reading fluency			
Difficulty decoding new words			
Poor knowledge of the sounds of words			
Spelling difficulty			

Frustration			
Attention and concentration difficulties			
Discrepancies between oral and written work			

3. Secondary/high school checklist

Characteristic	Frequency	Examples	Support needed
Takes a long time over homework			
Misreads words			
Poor general knowledge			
Takes longer than others in most of the class on written tasks			
May not write a lot in comparison to his or her knowledge on the subject			
Difficulty copying from books			
May not finish class work or examinations because he or she runs out of time			

Reflect on the checklists and in particular the support that might be needed – can the support be narrowed down to three or four areas such as decoding skills, spelling, memory work and comprehension? By narrowing in down it makes it easier to implement strategies and to monitor these over a period of time.

The importance of communication

Assessment is not the responsibility of any one person – it should be based on a whole-school approach. But the teaching assistant can have a role to play within that process particularly in relation to observation. Additionally, communication between home and school is extremely vital and again teaching assistants can play a key role in this. Parents can provide information on how their son or daughter deals with learning at home, their social skills and emotional maturity, memory, coordination and any area of confusion and anxiety.

Test results and implications

In this section we are not discussing specific tests, but rather the features of these tests and how the results can inform teaching.

Feature of test	Implications for the classroom
Rhyme recognition and rhyme production	
Alliteration tasks – ability to isolate initial sounds in words	
Naming speed	

Reading fluency – tests the speed of reading	
Working memory	
Long-term memory	
Omitting words when reading	
Substituting words when reading	
Non-word reading test	

From the implications for the classroom taken from the above chart it is possible to prioritize an action programme. Reflect on how useful this might be for an Individual Educational Programme (IEP)? What other kind of information may be helpful that is not included above?

Observation to support teaching

Behaviour to be observed	Possible responses	Possible interventions
Attention	Short attention span when listening	Short tasks with frequent breaks
Organization	Keeps losing items – not well organized	Needs structure – guidance and strategies to help with organization

Sequencing	Not able to put things in order, carry out instructions in order	Make lists, keep instructions short, try colour codes
Interaction	Preferred interaction – one-to-one? small groups? whole-class?	Try to ensure there is a balance of one-to-one, small group and class work
Expressive language	Meaning not accurately conveyed	Provide key points when discussing, do not ask open-ended questions, follow up answers with more specific questions
Are responses spontaneous or prompted?	Needs a lot of encouragement to respond	Identify strengths and allow the child to use these in different tasks
How does the child comprehend information?	Needs a lot of repetition	Use over-learning but try to make it varied so it is not too repetitive
What type of cues most readily facilitate understanding?	Needs a lot of visual cues	Ensure opportunities for illustrating answer – space out work on worksheets – visual images are important
What type of instructions are most easily understood – written, oral, visual?	Has difficulty with oral instructions	Ensure instructions are understood – need to be reinforced verbally

How readily can knowledge be transferred to other areas?	Has difficulty in knowing how to make connections with previous knowledge	Needs structure showing how new learning applies to previous learning
Reading preferences – aloud, silent?	Has difficulty in reading aloud	Minimize reading aloud in front of class
Type of errors	Note the type of errors he or she makes when reading aloud	See the next section on miscue analysis and the interpretation of reading errors
Difficulties in auditory discrimination	Inability to hear consonant sounds in initial, medial or final position	Use paired reading as it provides both auditory and visual feedback to the learner
Motivation level? Does child take initiative?	Reluctant to take initiative – needs a lot of prompting and not highly motivated	Encourage group work where responsibility is delegated so that everyone has a turn to be in charge
How is motivation increased, what kind of prompting and cueing is necessary?	Working with others seems to help	Make sure the group he or she is in is a positive experience. Experiment until you get the right group dynamics
To what extent does the child take responsibility for own learning?	Reluctant to do this – needs a lot of coaxing otherwise waits for the teacher to provide instructions	Meet the child halfway – provide a lead in and then get him or her to finish it but ensure there is constant monitoring

Level of self-concept?	Seems to have a low level of self-concept	Look for ways of giving the child some responsibility for their own learning – identify the strengths and highlight these, try to ensure that tasks are achievable
What tasks are more likely to be tackled with confidence?	Avoids writing but seems to be confident in practical tasks	Team up with writing buddy – balance writing with tactile and kinesthetic tasks
Is the child relaxed when learning?	Seems a bit stressed at times	Avoid too much pressure, allow more time for tasks – try to ensure that the learner manages to complete all tasks and does not fall behind
What are the child's learning preferences?	Seems to be visual and kinesthetic	Ensure that learning is experiential and that there are a lot of visuals

Try to make up a learning profile for the child based on the responses above – once you have done this reflect on how it might be used in the classroom.

Miscue analysis during oral reading

Miscue analysis is also based on observation. It investigates reading behaviours using curriculum-related text. The teaching assistant observes the child reading and records the type of errors in order to note any patterns. Often miscues occur systematically and occur whether reading is silent or aloud. The marking system that is usually adopted in miscue analysis is indicated below:

- **Omissions** – these may occur in relation to reading speed. As the child progresses in reading ability and reading speed increases, omissions may still be noted as they tend to increase as reading speed increases.
- **Additions** – these may reflect superficial reading with perhaps an over-dependence on context clues.
- **Substitutions** – these can be visual or semantic substitutions. In younger readers, substitutions would tend to be visual and in older readers contextual. In the latter case they may reflect an over-dependence on context clues.
- **Repetitions** – these may indicate poor directional attack, and perhaps some uncertainty on the part of the reader about a word to be read.
- **Reversals** – these may reflect the lack of left–right orientation. Reversals may also indicate some visual difficulty and perhaps a lack of reading for meaning.
- **Hesitations** – these can occur when the reader is unsure of the text and perhaps lacking in confidence in reading. For the same reason that repetitions may occur, the reader may also be anticipating a different word later in the sentence.
- **Self-corrections** – these would occur when the reader becomes more aware of meaning and less dependent on simple word recognition.

Top Tips!

It is important to observe whether the miscue is self-corrected. This means that the child is very likely comprehending what he or she is reading. It is, there-fore, possible to obtain useful data on the child's reading pattern by noting the self-corrections, observing the reading errors and noting the signifi-cance of these oral errors.

Linking assessment with support

It is important to focus on the child's actual performance when undertaking an assessment. This means that you are looking for a pattern of learning behaviours that can help you identify the strengths and weaknesses of the child. This will also help to inform your teaching.

Some of the difficulties children with dyslexia may experi-ence are shown below:

- difficulty in identifying the key ideas in information text
- difficulty in sequencing and arranging information in order
- difficulty in judging the importance of information and comparing it with other pieces of information
- over-reliance on a limited vocabulary
- difficulty remembering and recalling 'names' accurately, for characters and details in text
- difficulty spelling technical words, names and places
- difficulty learning factual details
- difficulty understanding abstract concepts,
- difficulty accurately drawing and labelling pictures and diagrams
- difficulty remembering and following instructions accu-rately and fully

- difficulty recording information accurately
- difficulty identifying the key questions to ask.

Some general suggestions to deal with these include:

- label charts and diagrams
- add pictures to text to enhance the meaning
- use colour to highlight key points
- use games to consolidate vocabulary
- use different colours of print or paper for different purposes
- combine listening and reading by providing text and tape or reading together
- use mind maps, bullet points and spider diagrams
- allow student to record their own reading and thoughts
- present information in small amounts
- using a variety of means to present information with frequent opportunities for repetition and over-learning
- reinforce learning by utilizing the visual and kinesthetic mode with video, films and field trips.

Some of these will be discussed in more detail in the following chapter.

Barriers to learning

It is useful therefore to view assessment and identification in terms of a process, and this process should focus on the barriers to learning rather than child-deficit factors. Both information on the child's cognitive skills and information from curriculum tasks are important.

This can be done through the use of curriculum-focused attainment objectives. This focuses on monitoring the child's learning behaviour from which the barriers to learning can be identified.

Reading behaviour

Try using the table below to monitor a student's reading behaviour:

Behaviour	Comment
Chooses to spend time looking at books	
Reads with other children	
Knows the difference between letters and words	
Understands the relationship between print and illustrations	
Shows understanding of the structure of text by retelling/ predicting content	
Identifies the letters of the alphabet in upper and lower case	
Likes hearing stories	
Forgets the beginning of the story and the names of the characters	
Needs a lot of time for reading	

Top Tips!

It is important to identify the reading behaviour of children. Reflect on some children you know and indicate how you can organize their reading programme to suit their current reading behaviour. You may also want to suggest some desired target behaviours that you feel the child should be aiming for.

The process of early identification – initial early warning signs

The class teacher and the teaching assistant may identify some behaviours through observation, such as coordination difficulties, difficulties with pencil grip, immature use of language and sequencing or organizational difficulties all prior to the teaching of reading skills. These difficulties can be identified through classroom observation, discussions with parents as well as diagnostic assessment.

Other points to look out for and discuss through consultancy include:

- difficulties in phonological awareness, such as awareness of rhyme, syllabification, natural breaks in speech and written language
- auditory discrimination such as recognizing and repeating sounds
- visual difficulties such as failure to recognize letters, comparison between visually similar letters, missing lines when reading confusing picture cues
- sequencing difficulties such as confusing order of letters, words or digits
- organizational difficulties such as directional confusion, laterality problems and sequencing difficulties
- memory – inability to follow instructions, particularly when more than one item needs to be remembered
- motor difficulties – for example, poor pencil grip, awkward gait, poor coordination, difficulty doing two simple tasks simultaneously.

Assessment/consultancy with school management

This is an important part of the process and time should be specifically allocated for this. This can involve:

- discussing the difficulties and possible materials and resources which can be used
- close monitoring of progress
- the time needed to develop new programmes and adapt current programmes
- how to feed back progress to parents and to other staff.

Assessing competence – multiple intelligences

It is important to make assessment a positive experience. Assessing competence should indicate not what the child **cannot** do, but what he or she **can** do!

One way of doing this is to utilize multiple intelligences, not only as a teaching guide but also to measure levels of performances through the child's preferred intelligences.

When Howard Gardner wrote *Frames of Mind* (1983) the concept of intelligence and its applicability to education had to be re-examined. Gardner assessed intelligence measures not through only assessing language abilities using paper and pencil tests, but rather in a multifaceted way. He suggested that the particular social and cultural context in which the individual lives can determine intelligence more than the notion of people having fixed human potential.

This means that measuring intelligence depends on the task and the culture, and it will have more flexibility and operate across a more comprehensive set of criteria than traditional assessment. According to Gardner this means that a significant part of an individual's intelligence exists outside his/her head, and this therefore broadens the notion of assessing intelligence to involve many different aspects of a person's skills, thoughts and preferences. Gardner accepts that intelligences do not work in isolation, but usually interact and combine with other intelligences. He suggests that everyone possesses these intelligences in some combination and we all have the potential to use them productively. This has clear implications for the classroom and indeed for children with dyslexia and the need to develop the intelligences in classroom activities. It is important therefore that the notion of multiple intelligences is incorporated into assessment.

The eight intelligences suggested by Gardner can be summarized as follows:

- **verbal/linguistic** – this involves language processing
- **logical/mathematical** – which is associated with scientific and deductive reasoning
- **visual/spatial** – deals with visual stimuli and visual planning
- **bodily/kinesthetic** – involves the ability to express emotions and ideas in action such as drama and dancing
- **musical/rhythmic** – is the ability to recognize rhythmic and tonal patterns
- **interpersonal** – involves social skills and working well in groups
- **intrapersonal** – involves metacognitive type activities and reflection
- **naturalist** – this relates to one's appreciation of the natural world around us, the ability to enjoy nature and to classify for example different species of flora, and how we incorporate and react emotionally to natural environmental factors such as flowers, plants and animals.

Each of these intelligences can be incorporated into assessment and can link to teaching. It is important therefore that the skills and preferences of children with dyslexia are utilized in a multiple intelligences curriculum. For example:

- verbal-lingustic – creative writing, poetry and storytelling
- logical/mathematical – logic and pattern games and problem solving
- visual/spatial – guided imagery, drawing and design
- bodily/kinesthetic – drama, role play and sports
- musical/rhythmic – tonal patterns and music performance;

- intrapersonal – thinking strategies, metacognition and independent projects
- naturalist intelligence – field work as well as projects on conservation, evolution and the observation of nature.

Multiple intelligences can therefore be used as a means of measuring and monitoring performances and success in different types of tasks. There is a preoccupation with performances being measured in a summative way at the end of a task. It is important that assessment should be seen as a means of monitoring as well as of measuring.

Formative assessment

Formative assessment is important as it can give a measure of success and provide the kind of feedback that is useful for the school and for parents. Unfortunately formative assessment is usually in the form of pen and paper exercises, which can discriminate against learners with dyslexia. It is important to look for alternative means of measuring competence. This could be done through:

- group presentations
- projects and field work
- posters and poetry
- investigation and reports on these investigations
- self-assessment
- practical demonstrations and models.

Obtain a programme that has been devised for a child with dyslexia. Reflect on how the programme can be adapted to incorporate multiple intelligences. Identify some activities from the suggestions above and try to work out how they can be incorporated into a classroom observation assessment.

Chapter summary

This chapter has been about identifying and assessing needs. This means that it is important to ensure that dyslexic characteristics are identified and that programmes of classwork are developed to acknowledge this. This needs to be acknowledged in the teaching approaches and also in the assessment. Assessing the child's performance is important and it is crucial that alternative means are considered to do this apart from traditional paper and pencil tests. This information could be obtained through observation as well as through more traditional tests. It might also be useful to consider multiple intelligences and how these can be incorporated into an assessment framework for children with dyslexia. The key point of this chapter is that assessment and identifying needs should clearly link with teaching approaches. Assessment needs to inform teaching and teaching assistants need to be aware of this. They can be instrumental in implementing teaching approaches based on the results of different forms of assessment.

Top Tips!

Self-assessment is important as it helps learners take responsibility for their own learning. This is an important factor in learning and particularly in developing comprehension and metacognitive skills. This can promote more reflective learning which is crucial in order to develop the learning potential and comprehension skills of children with dyslexia.

3

Supporting the learner

Children with dyslexia can learn more effectively if those who support their learning establish teaching practices which differentiate the material. There are many ways to do this and it does not necessarily mean preparing completely different material for every student. It does mean that in order to support the learner, we must develop an understanding of our students' needs. This includes the learning preference that makes them unique and allows them to take in and process information, and then to show that they have understood it. These points will build the foundation for this chapter. The key aims of this chapter are to show:

- differentiation – strategies and examples
- inferential learning – this cannot be assumed; teaching must be clear, direct and explicit particularly in the presentation of material
- the need for both teacher and learner to be involved in an active and interactive learning situation
- the need for all learning to be multisensory
- the need to give thought to how a student will access the material and whether or not it can be adapted in presentation to make it more accessible for the student
- the need to be mindful of specific goals when supporting reading
- how to teach spelling concepts explicitly.

Differentiation

This is the process of adapting materials, teaching practices and teaching environments to suit a range of learners' abilities and levels of attainment.

Ways to differentiate vary widely and will depend on the students individual learning needs. Some suggestions include:

- **Abridged books** – these are books that have been condensed or shortened. The language is simplified and some of the information that could be considered superfluous is taken out. In an abridged narrative the parts taken out are usually the bits of the story that provide extra information on the characters to make them more of a reality for the reader but don't affect the intention of the story. In a non-fiction text the abridged version would summarize the main points as briefly as possible.
- **Abridged workbooks** – these are often available to accompany a novel study. It is important to have a look at them to be sure the workbooks are still challenging to the students. Often the content is simplified and that is not always what is necessary for the dyslexic student. For some students, they may be better supported by adapting the questions yourself, making them more dyslexia friendly, by changing the text or rewording the question using simple sentences and easier language.
- **Audio books** – audio books are often available in both an abridged version and an unabridged version. The unabridged version is good if a student has poor reading

skills but wants to follow along with the text or wants to appreciate the book in its entirety. This can be extremely beneficial in helping to develop the child's language experience and extending their vocabulary as well as providing an insight into narrative and story plots. The abridged version is good for simply following the storyline and will of course be much quicker to finish. It can often cut the listening time down by 50 or 75 per cent of the time it would take to listen to an unabridged version. A number of resources for using taped books are shown in the appendix.

Top Tips!

When choosing a novel study, choose a book the student will be interested in. If possible, let the student be involved in choosing the book or choose a book that fits a particular theme you will be working on in another part of the curriculum. We are so fortunate to live in a world filled with great literature; the student will get off to a better start if they are excited about the book they are reading.

Presentation of material

It is important to give thought to how each student will access the material. Here are some of the accommodations you may consider when presenting material to students:

- **Font** – retyping in a larger, more dyslexic-friendly font such as Century Gothic can make it easier for students to read.
- **Paper** – use a different colour paper or different colour font. Some students are distracted by the glare of white paper.

- **Key points** – provide a list of key points using bullets.
- **Headings and subheadings** – the organizational structure can make it much easier for a dyslexic student to read and understand.
- Provide **mind maps**, spider diagrams and other organizational webs.
- **Highlight** key words or phrases.
- **Visuals** – add pictures to the text to aid comprehension.
- **Smaller amounts of information** - break information down in order to present it in chunks.

Accessibility of the task/content

There are a variety of ways to make tasks more accessible to learners. Sometimes it may be necessary to:

- Reword the directions or instructions with simple vocabulary, clear and short sentences in a logical sequential order. Keep the concept and ideas the same but change the vocabulary to be more easily understood.
- Read instructions, one step at a time, to the student.
- Adapt the task to fit the strengths of the student.
- Graduate the task from simple to more complex.
- Vary the activities or learning strategies to give the student alternatives to explore the content. For example they may use graphs or webs to show their comprehension of the concepts rather than writing a paragraph.
- Focus on the content of their writing rather than the spelling, punctuation and grammar.
- Environment – consider how the learning environment is affecting the student.
- Ensure the instructions are written in clear, simple, sequential steps so the student can follow as you are explaining.
- Visual aids – dyslexic students will often benefit from having plenty of visuals to support what they are learning. These can be in the form of photos, videos, museum

pamphlets or brochures, websites, or it may be very helpful to have the student create their own visuals by drawing, colouring, painting etc.

- Assessment – consider accommodations for tests, writing assignments, novel studies and in the classroom (accommodations versus modifications).

Dictionaries

It can be useful for the student to keep a personal vocabulary dictionary. It may save them the task of looking up the same word repeatedly if they cannot remember either the spelling or the definition. Second, it can help them when they are writing by keeping a list of descriptive vocabulary, synonyms for overused words (such as 'said') or words specific to an area of study. Picture dictionaries are also very useful – for some students it will really help them to sketch a picture to represent the words in their personal dictionary. They may like to add colour where or when it is appropriate, or if time permits.

Points to think about when planning a novel study

- Curriculum – how does the novel relate to the curriculum or something they may be learning about?
- Link the novel to background knowledge to enhance comprehension.
- Personal interests – is the student interested in the characters or the plot in the novel?
- Taped books – is the novel available in a taped version?
- Movie – has the novel been made into a movie? For some students it is very helpful to see the film before reading the novel.
- Have the student keep a sequence of events by chapter, event, or by beginning, middle and end. This can be done by using a mind map, an organized chart, drawings representing each chapter or event in sequential order (these can be done on 10 × 15cm cards) or by using a timeline.

- Keep character webs listing characteristics of major and/or minor characters.
- Create drawings or other visuals of the characters and settings.
- Family tree – if appropriate to the novel.

Points to think about when arranging groups

- Create discussion groups which will support the learner. Choose the students who will be in the group with care and acknowledgement of the students learning preferences.
- Partner students who can support each other (one who likes to do the writing with one who can't or would prefer not to).

Multisensory teaching and learning

- Use all the learning pathways in the brain: visual, auditory, tactile, kinaesthetic.
- Be sure the student is an active learner, participating at all times. This can be as simple as having them repeating sounds or spelling concepts after you, tracking while reading, asking questions during reading passages, tracing over letters or words.
- Change positions: try sitting on a ball, standing on a balance board, writing on a white board, lying on the floor, reading in beanbag chairs or on cushions on the floor.
- Play games to reinforce concepts.

Self-esteem (see also Chapter 8)

- **Making students feel normal** – most dyslexic students are tuned in to the fact that they are not doing what their peers are doing. It is important for them to understand that

Think of a concept that has been recently taught but the student may be having difficulty with the retention or application. Start with a blank game board and create a game that will reinforce that concept (see Appendix 2 for blank game board).

everyone learns differently and all students have different strengths and weaknesses. If we learn to teach them the way they learn, they will also be successful.

- Understanding their individual **learning style** – it is important for you to understand their learning style but it is as important for the students to understand how they learn best. They can start by filling out a simple questionnaire (see 'Learning styles' questionnaire in Appendix 1).
- **Stigma** – try attending to children's needs without making it too obvious. Find ways of supporting the student that don't single them out any more than necessary. Tell them quietly that you will be supporting their learning in a particular task.
- **Create an agreement** whereby if you move to stand directly in front of them it means you are aware they will need extra instruction and will give it to them as soon as appropriate (for example when the teacher finishes speaking).
- **Student-centred learning** – focus on the interests and strengths of the student rather than be directed too much by others, or the curriculum objectives. Start teaching where the student is in his or her learning, not from where the student should be.

Feedback

The feedback you give students should encourage and promote learning. Regular, positive feedback will motivate learners to continue. Praising your student is a good way to build confidence and raise self-esteem. Praise should be specific and genuine without a negative at the end. For example, avoid saying things like 'your penmanship was well done; too bad you don't write like that every day'. Rather, say 'you are really coming along with your penmanship, you did well today'. The negative at the end will cause the positive part of the comment to be disregarded. Students will want to do more of what they were praised for if the praise is genuine.

> Thinking of your students, make a list of phrases you can use that are specific in the praise you could be giving. They can include comments about their behaviour, organization, work habits, completed task or progress. Try to give a reason for praise, e.g. the slant of your penmanship improved today because you were keeping your paper at a really consistent angle.

Questioning

- **Open questions** – Ask open-ended questions as opposed to closed questions. Open questions could be: 'Tell me . . . ?' 'What might . . . ?' 'How will . . . ?' This helps the student to extend his or her thinking.
- **Closed questions** – these have a yes or no answer and could be followed by asking why they think this is so.
- **Reflection** – ask questions that will encourage the student to think about prior learning and link it to what is being currently learned. This encourages transfer of knowledge and helps the student develop concepts and ideas.
- **Try and stimulate thought** – sometimes students need to talk about their thoughts in order to make them more clear and they will need assistance in recalling information. You

could give them cues to set them off – try key words, key phrases or the beginning of sentences.

■ **Take small steps** – Rather than saying 'Do you remember . . . ?', break what you are asking into small steps and say 'Show me . . . ' For example, if the student struggles with the spelling of *moat* guide them through a series of questions until they get it right without you actually giving them the answer. Say 'show me the ways you know to spell the long vowel /o/ sound' (o as in go, oa as in boat and ow as in snow). 'Underline the spellings you will find at the end of a word' (o and ow). 'Circle the one of those you know which is a middle spelling' (oa). 'Where do you hear the sound /o/ in moat?' (middle). 'Now show me how to spell *moat*.'

Advocacy

Helping students with dyslexia to become aware of how they learn and giving them this self-knowledge can be beneficial for developing self-advocacy and self-esteem. It is important therefore to:

■ Give students an understanding of dyslexia – what it is and how it affects them.
■ Provide them with some knowledge of their learning style. This will enable them to use their own learning style when working on their own, which can facilitate independent learning.

Communication

It is essential to establish communication with everyone working with the dyslexic student as well as the parents or guardians. A strong learning team who communicates and provides regular feedback will aid in the student's success at school and at home. Following are some ideas that will help in maintaining a strong communication triangle between home, teacher and teaching assistant (communication with other learning-support people who work with the student may be necessary and should also be encouraged):

■ establish a common goal
■ create a team
■ build bridges between school and home
■ ask for regular feedback from the students, teacher and parents/guardians.
■ use a notebook between home and school to keep a log and encourage communication
■ use email to discuss any issues that may arise and include everyone on the child's learning team
■ schedule regular meetings to discuss progress, goals, IEPs, strategies, learning styles, behaviour.

Reading skills

There are many different skills to work on when you are supporting reading and therefore you should always have a goal in mind. Are you focusing on word attack skills, fluency, voiced expression, punctuation or comprehension? The strategies you use with your student as well as the reading passage you choose should change according to the skill you are working on. For example if you are working on:

Fluency

■ Choose a passage that is a level below the students ability.
■ Before reading, present any words or phrases the student may stumble on, have them written out separately on 10 × 15cm cards, for the student to read. When the student comes across them in the passage they won't be entirely new.
■ Show the student a phrase written on a strip of paper, have

them read it silently, put the strip down (so the student can't see) and have the student tell you what it said. This will help them understand that reading should sound like talking.

Punctuation

▪ Be sure the student has a clear understanding of punctuation. If the level of understanding isn't good, teach it explicitly before expecting them to demonstrate understanding of punctuation in a reading passage.

▪ Have the student tap the table (or their leg) every time he or she comes to a period, exclamation mark or question mark.

▪ Give the student reading passages that have a lot of quotations and take turns reading with voiced expression according to who is speaking.

Spelling

▪ Teach spelling rules explicitly and provide a lot of practice using the rules. Don't introduce exceptions to spelling rules until the rule has been mastered. Have the student demonstrate mastery by teaching the rule to you.

▪ Multiple spelling choices – be sure individual phonograms are secure before introducing a multiple spelling choice. Introduce the most common spellings first and then add the least common once the others are secure. Provide the student with concepts or rules for each of the spellings. Provide a lot of practice.

▪ Using codes – allow students to keep the code to spelling rules or spelling concepts on their desk or in their notebook. They can refer to the code when applying the spelling rule or spelling concept until it is secure.

▪ Key words and visuals – use key words and visuals when teaching and reinforcing spelling concepts. They can be used for phonograms and for rules and will help with recall and application.

■ Mnemonics and kinesthetic clues – dyslexic students may have difficulty recalling the spelling of non-phonetic words. Using mnemonics and kinesthetic clues will help the student with recall.

Reflect on the present practice of differentiation used in your classroom. Brainstorm ideas for teaching strategies you could use to differentiate more effectively.

Chapter summary

This chapter has provided insights and ideas on how to accommodate learners who are struggling with reading, spelling and writing. It has given teaching assistants a starting point from which they can decide what is best for their student and begin the task of making their material accessible. It is imperative to gain insight and understanding of students' needs and learning preferences. It is also necessary to equip the student with knowledge and understanding of their learning preferences in order for them to be supported in the methods that work best for them, while also working towards learning independently. Dyslexic students need explicit, multisensory teaching with materials which have been adapted to be dyslexia-friendly. They need to be actively involved in the learning process as this will increase the opportunities for effective learning and eventual success.

4

Planning for learning

It is important that teaching assistants are not simply viewed as 'hands-on' classroom support. They have an important role to play in the planning of learning as well as in supporting learning in the classroom. Usually planning takes place in collaboration with the teacher and other school staff. But at the same time it is important that teaching assistants understand the rationale underpinning educational plans and are also able to contribute to these plans, both in the collaborative situation and independently.

This chapter will focus on:

- the preparation of learning and teaching plans
- the type of consultation and information that is necessary to prepare plans
- supporting the child through the different stages of information processing including ten tips for developing information processing
- 20 pointers for planning.

Individual education plans

An individual education plan (IEP) is usually essential for a student with dyslexia. It can provide:

1. an analysis of a student's needs
2. the steps in a student's learning programme
3. a record of achievement.

These factors are crucial in order to ensure the teaching is at the right level and that effective learning is taking place.

Identifying needs

Before planning takes place it is important that accurate information is obtained on the child and that the information gathered is sufficient to inform the planning process. It is important to develop a framework to help with this. An example of a framework is shown below:

Framework for Planning

Information obtained from observation and interaction with the student

Student criteria	Comment
Learning style	Seems to be a visual learner, likes working in groups
Organization	Forgets equipment, needs a lot of reminders
Attention	Attends well when discussing and making something – difficulty in listening for more than two or three minutes
Reading accuracy	Has difficulty in blending, tends to read visually and confuses words that sound alike
Reading fluency	Hesitates a lot when reading – reads slowly
Spelling single words	Has difficulty with words with double consonants
Spelling in context	Confuses their and there and similar words – makes more spelling mistakes in written work

Expressive writing	Does not write a lot – knows more than he or she is able to write. Does not organize written work very well
Memory	Good long-term memory but forgets instructions readily
Comprehension	Needs a lot of explanation – often needs one-to-one explanation and has to be shown what to do with examples

It is important to obtain information from the student through observation and by asking the student questions about his or her learning preferences. It is also important to gather information that will assist in the development of the materials to be used in learning – books, resources, sources of information, as well as the type of tasks that are to be developed. Knowledge of the student's learning preferences can help to inform you when developing worksheets and programmes of work. Key points for gathering information on materials and tasks are shown below.

Information on material and task

Criteria	Comment
Font used – is it large enough and clear enough for the student?	
Vocabulary – is the vocabulary at the right level for the student?	

Learner-friendly – are there opportunities for revising and recapping on what has been learnt and opportunities for summing up?	
Interesting – will it hold the student's attention?	
Visuals – are there enough visuals to help the learner to follow the information?	
Is the task achievable – will the student succeed or will it be too challenging?	
Is it possible for the learner to investigate and find out more information without assistance?	
Are the instructions clear?	
Will the learner realize what the outcome of the task is supposed to look like?	
Is there a reward at the end of the task or is there some progression that the student is able to appreciate?	
Are there opportunities for the student to self-monitor and self-correct?	

Information processing

It is a common view that students with dyslexia have a difficulty in processing information. This needs to be taken into consideration when planning for learning. It is important to consider how information is received by the student (input) how it is learned, remembered and understood (cognition) and how the student can demonstrate that learning has taken place (output).

Learners with dyslexia can have difficulties at all these stages in the information processing cycle. It is worthwhile therefore to identify strategies for supporting students with dyslexia throughout these stages.

10 tips on supporting information processing

1. Identify the student's preferred learning style.
2. Present new information in small steps.
3. Utilize over-learning – use as wide a range of materials and strategies as possible.
4. Relate new information to previous knowledge.
5. Group, or chunk, information together to help learning to become more efficient.
6. Show connections between different pieces of information – learners may not be able to do this themselves.
7. Help learners develop their own memory strategies such as mind mapping, colour coding and mnemonics.
8. Help children identify the key points in new learning, or in a text.
9. Assist the learner to learn how to summarize information.
10. Measure progress orally as well as written – encourage discussion.

The contents of a plan

In order for an IEP to be used effectively it should include the following:

- details of the nature of the child's learning difficulties
- the provision to be made
- strategies to be used
- programmes, activities, materials
- any specialized equipment
- targets to be achieved
- the time frame for any specified targets
- monitoring and assessment arrangements
- review arrangements with dates.

Planning checklist – overview sheet

Child	Difficulty	Effect of difficulties	Comments
	Organization	Forgetting equipment	Colour coding notebooks, more reminders
	Spelling	Difficulty with spelling rules	Spelling programme, computer spelling game
	Sequencing information	Writing can be quite jumbled may not make sense	Provide writing frames
	Memory	Difficulty remembering facts	Provide insights into Mind Mapping

A planning checklist can be useful as a monitoring tool. It is also good to use information from an assessment here and this will provide a clear link between the assessment and teaching.

20 pointers for planning

1. **Small steps** – it is important, especially since children with dyslexia may have short-term memory difficulties, to present tasks in small steps. In fact one task at a time is probably sufficient. If multiple tasks are specified then a checklist can be a useful way for the child to note and self-monitor his or her progress.

2. **Group work** – it is important to plan for group work. The dynamics of the group are crucial and dyslexic children need to be in a group where at least one person is able to impose some form of structure to the group tasks. This can act as a modelling experience for dyslexic children – it is also important that those in the group do not overpower the dyslexic child – so someone with the ability to facilitate the dyslexic child's contribution to the group is also important. This would make the dyslexic child feel they are contributing. Even though they may not have the reading ability of the others in the group, they will almost certainly have the comprehension ability, so will be able to contribute if provided with opportunities.

3. **Use of coloured paper** – there is some evidence that different colours of background and font can enhance some children's reading and attention

4. **Layout** – the page layout is very important and this should be visual but not overcrowded. A coloured background is often preferable. Font size can also be a key factor and this should not be too small. In relation to the actual font itself it has been suggested that Sassoon, Comic Sans and Century Gothic are the most dyslexia-friendly fonts.

5. **Allow additional time** – some dyslexic children will require a substantial amount of additional time particularly for tasks like copying from the board and writing exercises.

6. **Produce a checklist to ensure instructions have been understood** such as – what is actually being said/asked? What is required of me? How will I know if I am right? Often dyslexic children do not get the right answer because they have not fully understood the task. Take time to ensure the task is fully understood before allowing the child to work independently.

7. **Put different types of information under different headings.** This can help with long-term memory and the organization of information.

8. **Provide key words** – this is crucial as often dyslexic children have difficulty in identifying key words. They may often go for the irrelevant aspects of a passage or provide too much information because they have this difficulty in identifying the key points.

9. **Use multisensory techniques** – visual, auditory, kinesthetic and tactile. This is important as it ensures that at least some of the activities will be tapping into the child's strong modality.

10. **Use mnemonics to boost memory** – this can be fun as well as an effective means of learning. It is best to personalize the mnemonic so encourage the child to develop his or her own mnemonic.

11. **Use of ICT to help with processing speed and learner independence.** There are a vast number of excellent ICT programs that can boost all aspects of learning (see Appendix 3). Computer programs can also help with learner autonomy.

12. **Make sure group dynamics are right and constructive for the dyslexic student.** This is important as group work can be very rewarding but only if the dyslexic child is in a constructive group. Try to ensure the group hasn't got too

many children who do a lot of talking – groups need listeners too.

13. **Use enquiry approaches** – to promote thinking skills. Problem-solving activities can be useful as often there is not enough reading before the problem can be tackled. Similarly with fact-finding tasks – these can also be motivating but ensure there is clear guidance on how to find the information. A child with dyslexia can waste a lot of time looking for information on the internet or in the library and may gather irrelevant information. It is important therefore to provide a clear structure for this.

14. **Use tape recorders to allow them to record their thoughts.** This can be good for helping with metacognition (that is, being aware of how one learns). By recording their thoughts on a tape it promotes self-thinking. They need to be aware of how they are actually tackling a task to be able to record their thoughts and this process helps with metacognitive awareness.

15. **Look for ways of boosting the learner's self-esteem.** This is essential and will feature again in this book (see Chapter 8). It is important that children's self-esteem is continually being built up as it will encourage them to take risks with learning where otherwise they may have given up. It is crucial therefore that tasks are designed to ensure the child will experience some success. It is through success that self-esteem is boosted and success comes if the task that is presented is achievable. This is why it is so important that the planning of tasks is given a high priority.

16. **Try to develop their ability to question and to ask the right kind of questions about the task.** This is important because it helps the child to understand the task if they know the right kind of questions to ask. This can be quite difficult and it is important that this is practised through pre-task discussion.

17. **Highlight the key points in text** and in photocopied sheets.

18. **Ensure instructions are short and clear.** It is best to provide a series of short tasks rather than one long one. This also makes it easier for the child to monitor their own progress.

19. **Use games to consolidate vocabulary** – game activities can be excellent for motivating students with dyslexia. Crossbow Education have an excellent range of games (www.crossboweducation.com). These include digital phonics, spingoes phonics activities, magic e spin it, knockout, and vowel digraph triplets (see Appendix 2).

20. **Try to develop creativity, thinking and problem-solving skills.** This is vitally important and is an area that is often overlooked when teaching dyslexic children because there is often a preoccupation with teaching literacy skills which can be at the expense of creativity.

Chapter summary

This chapter has:

1. Emphasized the importance of planning and preparation before new material is presented.

2. Indicated that the materials and the task need to be differentiated and considered in the planning as well as the individual challenges experienced by the student.

3. Provided some suggestions to help the student deal with difficulties in information processing.

4. Provided pointers to planning which can help all those involved in teaching anticipate the difficulties the student will likely experience.

5

Extending learning: comprehension, study skills and learning styles

It is important that teaching assistants have a full understanding of how children learn. Increasingly the role is becoming more skilled. This means that learners will require more direction from teaching assistants. It also means that teaching assistants will assume more responsibility for planning and implementing learning. It is crucial that teaching assistants have an understanding of the learning process and appreciate how that process can go wrong for some children.

This chapter will focus on the following:

■ the learning process
■ developing comprehension skills
■ the role of thinking skills
■ the use of learning styles in accessing the curriculum.

The learning process

It is important to acknowledge that learning is a process and this process takes place over time. This is necessary for an understanding of and for consolidation of new material that is to be learnt.

Some key points about learning:

- learning is a process
- learning requires a period of consolidation
- learning is more effective when the content is familiar
- using the material to be learnt in different contexts and over time increases the opportunities for retention and understanding
- intrinsic (within the child) factors as well as extrinsic (environmental) factors can influence learning
- learning is lifelong.

Developing and extending the learning process

Try these strategies:

- **Talk** – discussion is crucial for most children. It is an active form of learning and can also help the teacher monitor the child's understanding. It can be used both in learning and assessment.

- **Drama** – some learners can develop comprehension more effectively through active participation. This uses the kinesthetic (experiential) modality and this type of learning can be essential for some learners.

- **Drawing** – visual representation can be also essential for many learners – some can only learn visually so even the most basic of information may have to be presented in this format.

- **Listening** – all learners need to develop listening skills but for some this can be challenging. It is important that listening is given a high priority – it is equally important however that listening should be only for short periods of time and interspersed with other forms of learning, particularly discussion.

- **Role play** – one of the key points about developing learning skills is that learning should be personalized by the learner. This will make learning more meaningful and will help to develop comprehension skills. One way of achieving this is to develop imagination. Role play can be an excellent tool for developing imagination. It helps to facilitate children's creativity and furthermore can make learning individual. Additionally role play uses the kinesthetic modality and this experiential type of learning can benefit many learners.

- **Feeling** – it is important to recognize that learning involves the whole person; the emotional aspects of learning are important. It is important to establish any anxieties the child may be experiencing regarding the learning process.

Make tasks short and have a wide variety – tasks should also be presented in a multisensory way.

Anxiety prevention checklist
1. Is the learner fully aware of the requirements of the task?
2. Is the vocabulary at an appropriate level for the child?
3. Does the learner feel comfortable in the learning environment?
4. If working in a group, are the group dynamics suitable?
5. Is the task multisensory – with visual and kinesthetic activities as well as written ones?
6. Does the task build on the learner's successes?
7. Has the learner's previous knowledge of the task been taken into account?
8. Will immediate positive feedback to the learner be possible?
9. Does the learner appear anxious about the task (facial expression, body language)?
10. Is the task structured for the learner?

Reflect on how you can adapt the task based on the responses to the checklist above.

Reflection

Often we do not give learners sufficient time to reflect. Reflection is an important aspect of learning and it is crucial that learners are encouraged to do this. For many it may not come easily and the reflection will need to be structured for them.

Example of structured reflection

Before the task:

- What is our goal?
- What do we want to accomplish?
- What do we need?
- What resources do we need?
- What is our deadline?

During the task:

- How are we doing?
- Do we need other resources?
- What else can we do?

After the task completion:

- Did we accomplish our goal?
- Were we efficient?
- What worked?
- What did not work?
- Why did it not work?

Collaborating

Learning can be more enjoyable and more effective if there are opportunities for collaborating. Group work is important but it is also important to ensure that the group dynamics are positive for all the learners. Some children may feel intimated in a group while others can feel bored. It is important the signs of group anxiety or boredom are noted.

Feedback

This is an important aspect of learning as it can reinforce the learning process and positive feedback can help to develop confidence and help the learner take 'learning risks' with future learning.

Learning style differences

A key aspect of understanding learning is the need to appreciate that learners' show individual differences in how they process, understand and retain information. Some of the key factors in relation to this are shown on pages 86–7.

Pace of work

Most learners with dyslexia need additional time to complete tasks so it is important that this should be accommodated when developing a programme or worksheet. It might be useful to obtain some background information through observation of the learner's processing speed. At the same time some learners complete work too quickly. In this case it is a good idea to demonstrate how work can be checked. Some children have difficulty in checking their work as they are unsure how this should be done. It may be a good idea to provide these children with a 'checking' checklist to ensure they are able to use any additional time effectively and to ensure they have completed the task.

Checking checklist

Comprehension:

- ▦ Read through the answer.
- ▦ What was the question?
- ▦ Have you answered the question?
- ▦ In what way do you think you have answered it?
- ▦ Are there any parts of the question you have not answered?

Proofreading:

- ▦ Can you spot any obvious spelling mistakes?
- ▦ Do the sentences run in sequence?
- ▦ Check the paragraphs – does each paragraph stand up on its own?

Structure:

- ▦ Is there an opening paragraph that relates to the question?
- ▦ Is there a suitable conclusion?
- ▦ Does the text cover all the information you need?

Content:

- ▦ Is the information relevant?
- ▦ Can you think of any additional information?
- ▦ Have you made appropriate references?

Check through the homework or any other class notebook belonging to a dyslexic child and note any unfinished exercises – this will provide an indication if the pace of work is too fast for the child.

Developing learning skills

The intervention for children with dyslexia often targets literacy skills. This is understandable since this is often their main difficulty. It is important also to focus on learning skills.

There is some research (Tunmer and Chapman 1996) which suggests that children with dyslexia can have poor metacognitive awareness, which means they may select inappropriate strategies for learning. They also have difficulty in 'unlearning' bad learning habits once a method has been utilized over time. This can be noted, for example, while spelling a word the child may habitually misspell it even after the correct spelling has been shown to him/her.

It has also been noted that children with dyslexia can often use inefficient methods when solving problems. They may use for example many different steps to get an answer rather than use a direct route to solve the problem. In some mathematical problems children with dyslexia may take twice the amount of steps to get the correct response as other children (Chinn 2002). This means that they may lose track of what they are working on. This highlights the importance of developing effective learning skills and strategies at an early age. This can be achieved through the following:

- a programme of study skills
- discussion
- developing ideas and concepts
- utilizing learning styles.

It is important to focus on the development of learning skills for students with dyslexia. They may have difficulty in or need help with:

- identifying key points
- using efficient learning strategies
- developing metacognitive awareness
- unlearning inefficient methods
- taking a number of steps to get the correct response
- scaffolding and comprehension building exercises.

Study skills

There are many different ways of tackling study skills with young learners with dyslexia. Much depends on the age and learning style of the student. There are however some key factors that should be considered with students with dyslexia which are highlighted below.

Organization

It is important to spend some time assisting the learner to organize their learning. There are a number of strategies that can help with this – one of which is Mind Mapping®, since this technique not only utilizes visual skills but also helps the learner organize the information into groups visually. See the following websites for information on how to create Mind Maps® (www.jcu.edu.au/studying/services/studyskills/mindmap/howto.html and www.buzan.com.au). Also the book *Mind Maps for Kids: An Introduction* by Tony Buzan is very useful.

Creating a Mind Map

It is best to start with a topic that is familiar to the student, such as a sport, hobby or what they did at the weekend. The procedure could be as follows:

1. List everything you did at the weekend.
2. List all the people you saw at the weekend.
3. List five topics that cover what you did at the weekend such as leisure, shopping, home, schoolwork and sport.
4. Put the topics and the people into groups around the central theme of My Weekend.
5. Try to divide these groups further e.g. sport – watching sport and playing sport.
6. Use a visual image for each of the categories with different colours.

Key words

It is important to help children with dyslexia identify key words in a text – often they may miss these words or misunderstand their importance. Once the key words are identified then they can obtain some help in organizing these words into categories, ideas and themes.

Association

Try to place words, or pieces of text, together that have a common link. This will help children with dyslexia remember more information and be able to recall it in a more organized and structured manner – for example if they are recalling information about a famous battle, all the facts about uniforms, weapons, locations and the countries involved can be linked together. Often children with dyslexia need this link to be made obvious.

Concepts

If a learner has good conceptual understanding then he or she will have a good understanding of the features of a topic, or individual aspects of the topic. For example, they could have a good conceptual understanding of the theme of 'pollution' – this would mean they also have an understanding of the different facets that make up an understanding of the environment and global warming. This is highlighted in the example below:

Environment – Necessary Concepts

- Geographical features – such as polar ice cap
- Recycling
- Global warming
- Toxic waste.

Others can be added to this list as necessary, but the key point is that each of these facets need to be broken down into smaller topics and the link between them made clear.

This kind of topic can lend itself readily to a visual diagram – which the student can make, to show the link between each of the areas.

Visuals

Visuals are important for dyslexic learners – often they need to see the word or the idea before they can understand it. It is usually more effective if they develop their own visual aid as this can be more meaningful for them, however, it is the visual image that is important.

Metacognition

Metacognition means thinking about thinking. This puts the emphasis on learners to reflect on their learning and particularly the learning process they are engaged in. Students with dyslexia may have difficulty with this and need structure and guidance. A process that can be structured for learners with dyslexia may include the following:

1. Questioning – *'why, what, where, how'*.
2. Clarifying – *'I see, but what about this?'*
3. Understanding – *'Right, I get it now'*.
4. Connecting – *'I did something like this last week'*.
5. Directing – *'Okay, I know what to do now'*.
6. Monitoring – *'Maybe I should do this now – that doesn't seem to be correct'*.
7. Assessing – *'So far so good'*, *'I think I am on the right track'*.

This type of process keeps the learner on track and at the same time provides learners with the responsibility for their own learning.

Strategies for accommodating to learning styles

Sound

The use of music is important and for some essential – be careful to obtain the right type of music for the leaner. As a rule classical music such as Mozart is usually unobtrusive and can be relaxing.

Groups

There should be a balance between group working and students working on their own. It is important to consider the dynamics in a group and to ensure that the student with dyslexia is not overshadowed by others in the group.

Light

It is important to ensure that the students' preferences in relation to this are acknowledged – some students prefer dim light, and a small table lamp can make a real difference to these learners.

Reflection

Teach students how to reflect on their own learning – this can involve encouraging them to think aloud so they can identify and monitor their own learning process. Encourage learners to keep records of their own progress, which will empower them to take charge of their own learning.

Self-esteem (see also Chapter 8)

A student with dyslexia will be able to use their own learning style and learn more effectively if they have positive self-esteem. It is important therefore to identify opportunities to develop their self-esteem. Allowing them to use their own learning styles can help with this. But how can self-esteem be acknowledged within the teaching and learning process? Try including the following:

- Ensure that all the objectives that are set are achievable and that students recognize this.
- Make the student feel important and that his or her personal contribution to the class is important.
- Use the students name all the time when speaking to him/her.

- Point out positive aspects of the student's work first when assessing it.
- Allow students to make choices and praise them for the choice they have made.
- Display students' work.
- When a student asks a question try to indicate the positive points about the question (but try not to be patronizing).
- Vary the assessment strategies used in the class so that all students will be able at some point to use their preferred learning styles.
- Spend time discussing a difficulty with the students and try to show how the experiences can be used positively.
- Encourage students to experiment with their learning and to take risks – always praise the outcomes by indicating the positive factors.
- Ensure that the particular working groups that students are allocated to in class are constructive for them. It is worth while spending some time ensuring the group dynamics are right.
- Take an interest in the student as a person – discuss his or her interests and their life outside school.
- Use programmes such as circle time and other self-esteem programmes that involve developing social skills and collaborative activities.
- Integrate team-building exercises into the daily work of the class.

Developing memory and examination support

Whatever role is assigned to teaching assistants by the school it is almost certain they will be working closely with students. The good point to emerge from that is that they will be in a position to assist learners in developing appropriate learning strategies. This is important as often students with dyslexia have difficulty in selecting the best strategies to help them understand and memorize information. Therefore it is important to:

- Provide guidance to teaching assistants who are in a position to work closely with students, both young primary-aged students as well as those nearing high school or secondary school examinations.
- Provide some suggestions for helping the student with examination support.
- Provide guidance to those working with younger learners who need a structure to their learning to help with comprehension and memory.

It is important to provide some study skills support for students with dyslexia of all ages as they may spend a lot of time and effort studying and revising for very little return. It is important to help them develop efficient methods of study that can help them to use their strengths.

Chapter summary

The chapter has looked at the importance of focusing on the development of learning skills for students with dyslexia who may have difficulty in:

- identifying key points
- using efficient learning strategies
- developing metacognitive awareness
- scaffolding and comprehension building exercises.

It is important to extend the learning skills of students with dyslexia and provide them with study skills support. Students with dyslexia may spend a lot of time and effort studying and revising for very little return. It is important to help them develop efficient methods of study that can help them to use their strengths. Teaching assistants may have more opportunities to get to know the learner through working closely with him or her and this can bring dividends in helping learners with dyslexia personalize learning strategies to help them become more efficient learners.

6

Support across the curriculum

In both primary and secondary school sectors, teaching assistants need to be knowledgeable in a range of curricular activities. Some areas of the curriculum such as mathematics and science require specific skills and often knowledge of subject-specific vocabulary, which can be challenging for pupils with dyslexia. This is the case in primary schools as well as secondary schools. Other subjects such as physical education, history, geography and music all have demands that can be challenging for students with dyslexia. This chapter will therefore focus on the following:

- supporting the student in mathematics
- assisting with physical education
- overcoming the demands of social subjects
- dealing with difficulties in music and art
- facilitating creativity in design and technology
- developing the role of drama in the curriculum.

The difficulties with mathematics

Symbols

Understanding and remembering symbols to many children with dyslexia represents learning a new language. It is important that time is taken to allow students with dyslexia to get to know the symbols, even basic ones such as multiply and divide.

Allow more time and ensure mastery before moving on.

Quantity

Much of mathematics is about understanding and using quantities and solving problems based on the relationships between these quantities. This can be demanding for students with dyslexia.

Ensure 'over-learning' takes place so that they can immediately recognize the different quantities – practise putting them in rank order with the biggest first and then reversing this, placing the smallest first; make up games based on quantity.

Organization

Students with dyslexia often get muddled when doing mathematics problems because their working is spread all over the page. They often take more steps to solve a problem than some other children so will need space for this, however many mistakes are made because the page is crowded.

It will be time well spent at the beginning of a task to ensure they have space on the page for the working and it might be useful to help them to organize the page. Additional working, such as additions, can be done at the side of the page clear of the main problem being calculated.

Rules and sequences

There are many rules and sequences in mathematics and remembering these can place a burden on the child with dyslexia. It is important these are consolidated in long-term memory, but to remember these effectively it is best if learning takes place in context.

It is a good idea to have a separate notebook for the rules they have to remember, which learners can refer to as they are using them. It is only through using the rules in context that they will be consolidated into long-term memory. Practise placing procedures in sequence and number or colour code each sequence – you could use traffic light sequences such as red, amber and green for one, two and three.

Poor recognition of shapes

This can be a problem for students with dyslexia. Some have good visual spatial skills but many have not, especially if the shapes are not meaningful for the learners.

Again it can be a good idea to have a separate notebook for the different shapes that are used, such as 'polygon' and 'hexagon'. This can be a small notebook they can carry about with them that will have the common shapes and they can use it as a reference. This is also a good way to build up automaticity. It is also a good idea to put the number of sides next to each shape.

Reading and vocabulary

Students with dyslexia can find mathematics difficult because of the reading that is associated with the task. Often it requires copying numbers and the copying as well as the reading can prove problematic. When copying they may also lose their place on the page.

Use simple vocabulary when presenting mathematics problems – it might be an idea to go over the sum or problem with the child before they start to tackle it to ensure they have copied it down correctly and that they have understood the instructions. It is useful to use some form of concrete aid as a marker to ensure they do not lose their place on the page.

Reversals of numbers and confusions of letters and words

This can be quite common especially with younger children. They may also confuse letters and words that look and sound similar.

Minimize copying by providing the sum for the child but copy it lightly. This will ensure the number is made correctly but it will provide the opportunity for the child to trace over the numbers him or herself. This will strengthen the kinesthetic memory.

Confusion of directional and place words

Students with dyslexia often confuse words and concepts such as left from right, up and down, back and front, before and after.

Try to use colour coding with a key for the student to see which colour represents which word (Reid and Green 2007).

Slow pace of work

It is well established that students with dyslexia can have difficulties with processing speed. Therefore their pace of work might be slow and extra time needs to be allowed for this.

Try not to place time demands on the child as this will cause some anxiety and exasperation, and exaggerate the difficulties he or she has with mathematics. Once the process has been mastered then the time factor can be introduced in an attempt to speed up processing. This can also be made into a game activity. Some computer games can be good for developing processing speed.

Attention and concentration

Mathematics can demand intensive attention over a period of time. This in itself can be demanding for children with dyslexia.

Try to break the task down into small units or chunks. Try to make the breaks quite natural so the flow of the problem is not disrupted too much. It might be important here also to find out the child's learning style, especially whether they prefer working in silence or with background noise. This can make a difference to concentration.

Frustration and anxiety

It is easy for a child with dyslexia to become frustrated with mathematics. This frustration can also produce fatigue and a feeling of 'learned helplessness'. They may then become anxious at the very thought of doing mathematics and this in itself becomes a hurdle to overcome. It is best to try to prevent this from happening.

Try to make mathematics a game and use visuals as much as possible. It might also be worthwhile spending time with the child in 'paired maths' where the first few problems are tackled together and then the adult gradually lets the child take the lead. Again it needs to be remembered that mathematics may be tiring for the child and short tasks and frequent breaks may prevent fatigue.

Poor visual tracking and visual acuity

This can be a problem because some children with dyslexia have visual difficulties and may miss lines or misread numbers because of these problems.

> Use coloured paper instead of white paper – this can be less of a contrast and easier on the eyes than the contrast between black print and white paper. Transparent colour rulers are also useful and can help with tracking.

Learning styles in mathematics

Mathematics is a very challenging subject for students with dyslexia so it is important that they are aware of their learning preferences as this will help them access challenging materials more easily.

Chinn (2004) identifies two types of mathematics learning styles – inchworms and grasshoppers.

The inchworm is the student who takes one piece of information at a time and places a heavy emphasis on sequence and the procedure. On the other hand the grasshopper is less likely to rely on sequence and tends to be a more random, and perhaps more unpredictable, processor of information. Many students with dyslexia tend to be grasshoppers. The result of this is that often they are unsure how they came to an answer and may find it more difficult to retrace their steps.

It is important therefore to help grasshoppers organize their work into a sequence and to help them identify the steps they are using. It is also important to support them in using their learning style more efficiently. That does not mean one has to try to change the style – just help them use their style in an efficient way. For example the grasshopper style is the most vulnerable in mathematics because it is a random style and mathematics is a precise and often sequential subject that requires strict adherence to processes and rules. The grasshopper learner would therefore require a structure to prevent them from going too far astray. At the same time the inchworm may take a long time to complete the problem as he/she may go through a very sequential and laborious route. Again this may be improved by checking to see if some of the steps can be omitted or shortened.

It is important to identify the student's learning style in mathematics as this can help you understand how they are attempting to solve the problems and where they may be going wrong. While it is important to try to make the style more effective and efficient for learning it is also a good idea to accept the learner's style, so do not try to change a grasshopper to a inchworm or vice versa.

Support in physical education

Physical education can provide an outlet for students with dyslexia to excel – some well-known athletes, for example Sir Steve Redgrave the Olympic rower, claim that being able to excel in sport was their saving grace as they found reading and other academic subjects very challenging.

At the same time it is important to appreciate that not all students with dyslexia have an aptitude for sport. Some in fact can have coordination difficulties and may find sport both frustrating and challenging.

It is important therefore to realise that some children with dyslexia will need support in PE.

Portwood (2004) claims that physical education is in fact a crucial area for developing motor and coordination skills, and it is an area that is sometimes neglected in relation to its value in developing cognitive and other learning skills, which applies particularly to children with dyslexia. Children with difficulties such as spatial awareness, rhythm, timing and visual processing can be supported in PE and this can have an impact in other subjects. This emphasizes the need to deal with dyslexia across the whole curriculum. The key text for this area is *Dyslexia and Physical Education* by Madeleine Portwood (see references).

Physical education – challenges and suggestions

Challenges	Suggestions
Hand/eye coordination	Try one hand catching – this might be harder, but all ball games can be good for developing hand/eye coordination. It might be a good idea to start with sponges or softballs first and then progress to other types of balls.
Being left out of team games	Best to try to prevent this from happening as the effects can be difficult to reverse. Try to prevent too much peer selection of teams.

Forgetting equipment	This is quite normal for many dyslexic children. Ensure they have a checklist of materials they need for the next day – the list can be colour coded, such as red for important.
Being late and slow in getting ready	You could put children in pairs so they can assist the other in getting ready for PE. It might be the child is slow in getting ready because he/she is reluctant to go to PE, and they may well benefit from some peer encouragement.
Balancing activities	This can be challenging for children with dyslexia – it is an idea to pair them up with someone who has quite good balance and they can help each other. It is also a good idea to get them to practise balancing by looking in the mirror as it gives them an idea of the movements they need to make to restore balance.
Jumping and hopping	This can be quite challenging because it requires both timing and coordination. Try using a small trampoline first to practise balance and to try out jumping and hopping. It is an idea to get the child to hold a large ball close to his/her chest to keep the arms down. This can help them maintain balance better while practising hopping.

The demands of social subjects

One of the key aspects about social subjects is that there is usually a considerable amount of writing associated with them. History in particular can have a lot of both reading and writing. It is important to try to make this as dyslexia-friendly as possible. Some suggestions are given below.

Strategies for social subjects

Writing

It is often necessary to use writing frames. These provide structure and guidance so students can follow the sequence of what they are writing and extend the content. Often students do not perform at the same level in written work as they do orally. It is also important to emphasize that spelling is not important in this context. To help to extend writing it is an idea to provide students with around six pictures and get them to make comments on each – the comments could then form the main points of the written work.

Reading historical information

This should be seen as more of an investigation and less of a reading exercise. It is important therefore to present the information in small pieces and discuss each piece with the student one bit at a time. It is also important to write out the key points after reading each piece. These can be done at the side of the page. This means that all the key points can be noted at a glance and this makes it easier to draw connections between them. It is also important to emphasize the purpose of reading, that is to gain key pieces of information, and this should be highlighted rather than the reading accuracy aspect.

Sequencing information

This can be problematic for the dyslexic learner and in history in particular it is usually important to understand and retain information in sequence. It might be a good idea to use paper with numbered squares or to use a time line.

Discussion

It is important to ensure children with dyslexia are not left out of discussions – often they can perform well in discussions but they may need time to gather their thoughts and to find the most appropriate words. Discussions are better when they are not abstract for children with dyslexia, it is best to make them concrete – encourage them to bring in old photos or objects and these can be the basis for their contribution to the discussion.

Vocabulary

It is important that the student has a good grasp of the vocabulary that is needed. It is important to keep vocabulary simple in worksheets and to make a glossary of key words and terms. It is an idea to get a student with support to make up his/her own glossary.

Categorizing information

There can often be so much information in subjects like history that organizing information can be a real challenge for the learner with dyslexia. It can be helpful to present information in chunks with some description attached to the information. This helps the learner categorize it which helps with both understanding and recall. It also helps with 'schema development', that is, the development of ideas and related vocabulary associated with the topic, which is necessary to develop concepts and higher-order thinking skills.

Map work and diagrams

Map reading in geography can be challenging for dyslexic children as can interpreting diagrams and graphs – it is important to use colour as far as possible to distinguish between different parts of a graph and to annotate each diagram so the student can understand the diagram with the aid of the text. Maps should be kept simple and it is important the student has a good understanding of the key to the map before working independently on map work.

Investigation

This is a major part of social subjects and certainly an area where the student with dyslexia can perform well. They may have good problem-solving skills but may have difficulty in carrying out the investigation due to the need to plan and sequence the process, as well as the demands of identifying the appropriate resources. It is a good idea to provide them with a work plan indicating the procedure and the resources that are necessary. It will be necessary to give them some direction regarding the reading – copying some document abstracts in history, for example, may be helpful. It is also a good idea to highlight the key points.

Assessment

It is important to try to make the assessment as varied as possible. Do not rely solely on written work to assess the students understanding and knowledge. Use other means, such as poetry, drama, visual stories and discussion.

Memory

Social subjects can have heavy content with a lot of information to remember. This can place some strain on the memory. It is necessary to provide the dyslexic student with strategies for developing their memory skills. These should be strategies they can personalize themselves, so that essentially they are developing their own strategies. What can be provided to them is some guidance on how to develop a more effective memory, such as below.

Guidance on developing an effective memory

1. *Chunking* – Place all similar pieces of information into one group – for example if the student is studying the geography of a country get him or her to make a chunk of all the facts relating to climate. Students should be able to chunk at least four items together so they should find at least four items that have a strong connection.

2. *Visualization* – Remembering information will be easier if learners can use all their senses when learning. This means using the visual modality and for some learners this is very important. A graphic or a symbol can help to strengthen the memory.

3. *Making connections* – It is important that dyslexic students make connections when learning. This makes learning meaningful and aids understanding and development of concepts. An effective learner is one who is able to make these connections. The key connection to make is that between previous learning and new learning. Questions the learner needs to consider are – is there anything about the new learning that is familiar? What is familiar and why? This will help learners connect between the previous and new learning and make learning more effective.

4. *Imagination* – It is a good idea to get students to use imaginative images or connections as these can stamp personal identity on the information to be remembered. By using their own images students can make information personal and this can aid memory.

5. *Repetition* – It is unusual to remember information first time around, but rote repetition is not always effective. When getting students to repeat information try to suggest a range of different ways they can recall it. Students can do this by using memory cards, visuals, headings, summaries, notes and discussion. All these can be used for repeating the same information. Students with dyslexia need a lot of 'over-learning' before they can consolidate new material.

6. *Understanding* – Understanding is vitally important for memory. Time taken to ensure the information is understood is very worthwhile. Teaching assistants can check understanding by asking questions about the information that is being learnt such as, Why? What? When? How? and So what then? If learners can answer these type of questions then it is likely they will have some understanding of the topic

7. *Discussion* – For some learners with dyslexia discussion is the only way in which they can retain and understand information. Discussion can make the information more meaningful and can help the learner experiment with ideas and views. It is this experimentation that helps the learner extend their thinking and learning. For some learners discussion can be like thinking aloud and this should be encouraged.

Top Tips!

Understanding is the key to an effective memory and oral discussion can help the student with dyslexia understand and remember the information more effectively.

Dealing with difficulties in music and art

Both music and art are subjects that students with dyslexia can do well in – both can utilize creativity and right-hemisphere skills. Some students with dyslexia can have significant strengths in these areas. Yet both require a degree of reading accuracy. This in itself can provide a barrier even if students have skills in music and art. It is important that the literacy barriers do not prevent them from reaching their potential in these areas.

Music – challenges and strategies

Challenge	Strategies
Reading of music scores. This can be like learning a new language. Students have to learn the meaning of symbols, some with only subtle differences between them and know when and how to use these symbols	Use colour as much as possible to distinguish between the different types of notes
Visual processing – convergence difficulties	Use coloured paper or coloured overlays
Eye tracking difficulties	Enlarge a normal-sized score
Speed of processing difficulties	Present the music score in short sections
Coordination difficulties	Allow the student to practise the instrument first before reading the music
Frustration	Emphasize that there is no competition, set small achievable targets

Art and design – challenges and strategies

Challenge	Strategies
Inability to see the detail of a painting	Use viewfinders to narrow down the perspective on a chosen painting
Remembering the styles of different artists	Use themes such as line and movement (Van Gogh), hues and shades (Monet), pattern and shape (Klimt), distortion and bold colours (Picasso)
Understanding the artist's motives and feelings	Visits to galleries looking at the biographical details of the artists are helpful. Use audio aids at galleries to obtain this information. Back in class bring these up in circle time to try to understand the artist's feelings and mood
Misconceptions of craft and design as a school subjects – many feel it is not academic, only practical	Educate staff that there can be a heavy reading content in design and this calls for a great degree of accuracy
Following sequential instructions – many of the instructions in design and technology can follow a sequence necessary for the product to be completed properly	Present the instructions one at a time. Ensure one stage is successfully completed before the student moves on to the next stage

Technical vocabulary – many new and unfamiliar words will be used in art and design technology, this can be demanding for the student with dyslexia	Get the student to develop a personalized dictionary. This should include the technical words with the meaning and if possible an illustration
Complex diagrams and instructions – even pictorial instructions can be complex	Ensure that each component of the diagram is annotated. This will help the student identify the pieces and see where the different components fit into the whole

Facilitating creativity in design and technology using multiple intelligences

Multiple intelligences can be usefully employed to ensure that a range of strategies are being used to help the student access the full curriculum. These have a cross-curricular role and can be used in all subjects. The table below shows how multiple intelligences can be used in design technology.

Intelligence type	Characteristics	Design and technology – strengths for dyslexic learners
Visual/Spatial Intelligence	Puzzle building, understanding charts and graphs, sketching, painting, creating visual metaphors and analogies (perhaps through the visual arts), manipulating images, constructing, designing practical objects, interpreting visual images.	Designing and producing a portfolio. Designing new concepts.

Verbal/ Linguistic Intelligence	Listening, speaking, writing, explaining.	Explaining concepts or answers to questions without writing it down. Working in pairs/groups.
Logical/ Mathematical Intelligence	Ability to use reason, logic and numbers, performing complex mathematical calculations, working with geometric shapes.	Working drawings and design concepts. Provide time to develop working drawings.
Bodily/ Kinesthetic Intelligence	These learners express themselves through movement. Experiencing the physical process of a task enables them to remember and process information.	Hands on experience of practical tasks will provide excellent ways in which to remember manufacturing processes.
Musical/ Rhythmic Intelligence	Whistling, playing musical instruments, recognizing tonal patterns, composing music, remembering melodies, understanding the structure and rhythm of music.	Memorizing information using a poem or rap can help jog the memory in an exam. An example of this could be a rhyme about the parts on a metal lathe.
Interpersonal Intelligence	Seeing things from other perspectives (dual-perspective), cooperating with groups, noticing people's moods, motivations and intentions.	Designing for specific target markets. Seeking out business ventures as a game – launching new products.

Intrapersonal Intelligence	These learners try to under-stand their inner feelings, strengths and weaknesses.	Evaluating products, reviewing the speci-fication and the quality of work. Use a game show approach to host a competition on new designs.
Naturalistic Intelligence	Studying in a natural setting, learning about how things work. Categorizing, preservation, and conserva-tion.	An affinity with materials. Curious minds for construc-tional work. Showing how envi-ronmental friendly products can be used to replace current products.

(adapted with permission, F. Renaldi (2005))

Developing the role of drama in the curriculum

Drama is a subject that can have cross-curricular implications. Eadon (2005) shows this by indicating that drama can enable students to understand themselves and others, extend literacy skills, develop teamwork and foster communication skills, aid problem solving and decision making, build self-esteem and confidence and explore issues and experiences in a safe and supportive environment.

Drama can present some challenges to students with dyslexia as it can have a heavy reading content, lines have to be memorized and performed in a specific order, however it can also be a really useful subject for facilitating creativity in the student with dyslexia. Games and role play can be developed on any subject, preferably using the students own experiences from a holiday, holiday snap or an incident or event recently seen.

Eadon suggests the use of a freeze frame to extend role play. A suggestion is to get the students into groups of four. One of them works for a local paper, or TV company in a seaside town that is very short of news at the moment. The student's task is to go to the beach and interview some tourists. The rest of the group are the tourists. The students decide on the most newsworthy item and perform that as a freeze frame. Drama can inspire creativity through improvisations – some suggestions for titles for spontaneous improvisations are shown below.

Titles to inspire or challenge students

Quick Change	Excuses	Wanted: Trainee
No Smoking	Excuse me, but could you . . . ?	Change in status
Waiting	Engaged	Help!
Stuck	Keep off the grass	Not again!

Chapter summary

This chapter has looked at the demands of a number of different areas of the curriculum and shown that these are applicable to both primary and secondary education. Many of the demands can be seen in more than one subject and have cross-curricular implications. There are whole-school staff development implications here but this type of awareness is not widespread and some teachers have little knowledge of the subject needs of students with dyslexia, particularly in secondary school. This also has implications for the training of teaching assistants. The teaching assistant therefore may need to inform teachers of the specific needs of some dyslexic students.

This chapter has also highlighted the challenges of subjects in which the student with dyslexia can do well, provided they are supported to help overcome some of the barriers to learning that they are confronted with. These barriers certainly include literacy but also include other factors such as memory, sequencing, organization and writing skills. This chapter also includes some suggested strategies for supporting the student with dyslexia across the curriculum, but it is important to individualize as far as possible these strategies for the individual student. Teaching assistants, who may have a better knowledge of individual students than some subject teachers because of the nature of their role, particularly in secondary school, are in a good position to carry this out.

7

Self-esteem and motivation

There is a great deal of research that suggests that learners with dyslexia may experience low levels of self-esteem. It is important that the teaching assistant is aware of the need to develop self-esteem and how this can best be achieved. It is also important to recognize the signs that a child has low self-esteem.

This chapter will look at:

- What is meant by self-esteem?
- Criteria for identifying children with low self-esteem.
- Strategies for developing positive self-esteem.
- The role of emotions in learning.
- Examples of positive motivation and reinforcement.

What meant by self-esteem?

Self-esteem is different from simply being confident – some very confident people have actually low self-esteem. Self-esteem can be equated more with security. It is essentially one's own estimation of oneself. This estimate can be altered depending on the feedback the person receives. Positive feedback can result in positive self-esteem. It is important therefore that children with dyslexia receive positive feedback.

It is important to acknowledge the role of self-esteem in learning. The damage that can be done to a child through low self-esteem may well be far greater than that done by neglecting educational progress. Low self-esteem can de-skill the child and undermine his or her confidence. This could result in a reduction in motivation.

Positive self-esteem is important at every stage of learning and children who have low self-esteem can become obvious soon after commencing school. It is crucial that teaching assistants are aware of the importance of self-esteem and how to identify children who may have low self-esteem. Often reluctance to undertake a task can be mistaken for disobedience and difficult behaviour when in fact it can be due to low self-esteem.

Children who act confident may actually have low self-esteem. It is important that this is considered when planning work for a child with dyslexia. Raising self-esteem could become a number one priority in planning and implementing a teaching programme for a dyslexic child.

Recognizing low self-esteem

Not all of the factors below can be a consequence of low self-esteem but together a number of these factors can point towards low self-esteem as an explanation of challenging behaviour or reluctance to work in class:

- Shows reluctance to apply him or herself to classwork.
- Can 'act-out' in front of class to get attention – be the class clown.
- May avoid people and isolate themselves from the class.
- Shows reluctance to display work.
- May take a deliberately long time to work out answers.

- Can appear defensive or argumentative.
- May be anxious when working.
- May be over careful in checking work.
- May avoid eye contact.
- Can be isolated from peers or seek out younger children.

Just as it is important to identify if the child is suffering from low self-esteem, it is also crucial to reflect on some strategies that can be used to raise self-esteem. There is no one way for all – much depends on the individual and his or her strengths and weaknesses as well as background experiences. Often children's level of self-esteem is already quite well established before they enter school. However, initial experiences at school can have a significant effect on the child, and children with dyslexia can be particularly vulnerable because often their early experiences are characterized by failure, since print and learning the foundations of literacy are important features of early education.

Raising self-esteem of children who are finding it difficult to grasp basic literacy skills should be a priority at an early stage in education. It should be an ongoing practice and it is important to be aware of strategies that can be effective in enhancing self-esteem.

Ten strategies for developing positive self-esteem

1. **Success** – this is important as success can help children with low self-esteem believe that they can do a task. This will also increase motivation. It is important to look for ways in which success can become a reality. This may not always be easy and often one has to review what is actually

meant by success. It could be that for some children with dyslexia success needs to be measured in a different way from that of other children. The important point is that the child needs to recognize that he or she has been successful.

2. **Being part of a group** – this can work to the child's advantage if the group dynamics are positive. It is important to take time to ensure the composition of the group is favourable for the child.

3. **Ensure tasks are achievable** – if the child repeatedly fails tasks then this will lower motivation and consequently affect their self-esteem. Try to avoid providing tasks that are ambiguous or too demanding.

4. **Recognize individual needs** – it is important to value the child as an individual – using names is important – especially in secondary or high school where a teacher can have several hundred children over the period of a week. If the child is valued as an individual them he or she will begin to appreciate that and this can have an impact of their feeling of self-worth and self-esteem.

5. **Identify strengths** – children will begin to believe in themselves if they are able to utilize their strengths. This will give them positive reinforcement and help to generate motivation as well as positive self-esteem.

6. **Delegate responsibility** – some children with low self-esteem can respond well to a degree of responsibility. This is important and effort should be made to look for situations where this can be possible.

7. **Display children's work** – this can have a really positive impact on some children – work should be displayed as much as possible.

8. **Playground buddies** – peer-group friendships can be important to all children. They can be extremely important for children with dyslexia as often their difficulties in the classroom may make them feel different from other children and isolated.

9. **Peer tutoring** – working with one other child can be beneficial for the child with dyslexia but it is important that the dyslexic child does not always feel like the learner – it is good to find some area where he or she can actually be the tutor in paired tutoring.

10. **Positive communication with parents** – there is a great deal of research showing the impact of parent's views and beliefs on their children. It is crucial that a positive message on the child is given to parents. This will transfer to the child and in terms of 'significant others' the parents rank at the top for most children.

Positive self-esteem	Negative self-esteem
Attention	Ignoring person
Praise	Criticism
Respect	Not respecting views
Friendships	Loneliness
Success	Failure

It can be clearly noted from the list and table above that it is not too difficult to look for ways of boosting the self-esteem of children with dyslexia. It is also a good idea to get the child him or herself to take some responsibility for developing their own self-image in a positive way. This would allow them to accept challenges and to feel secure in their learning experience.

The hidden effects of dyslexia

Dyslexia is a condition that may not be obvious all the time. Some children with dyslexia can be quite accomplished at covering up and pretending to be able to do something when in fact they are not managing the task well. Often children with dyslexia can be good in discussion. This can create an impression that they have an understanding of the topic, but they may not be able to display that in writing. Yet in terms of their oral presentation one can assume that they are entirely competent in the area. What one finds however is that children with dyslexia are often aware of their own difficulties and shortcomings and it is this that can lead to low self-esteem. It is important for the teaching assistant to appreciate this and to follow up children's responses to ensure the topic is fully understood. It is also a good idea to ensure they understand the task before leaving them to work independently. They may appear to understand but this can be deceptive. It really is crucial to go over the task with them orally first and then get them to repeat to you what they have to do.

Often one of the hidden effects of dyslexia is in fact a reluctance to ask questions at all, as the child with dyslexia may not want to appear that he or she isn't understanding the instructions or question to be tackled. For that reason it is good practice to take time to go over the task orally and to ensure that there is some form of monitoring at regular intervals to ensure the child is still on target to complete the task.

The role of motivation

Self-esteem can link to motivation and motivation is essential for successful learning. Additionally motivation can be an indication that students are assuming responsibility for their own learning. It is quite common to begin to motivate a learner through the use of extrinsic motivation. That is usually seen in rewards being offered that can be appealing for the learner – this might be sufficient bait for the child to be motivated to achieve the task Often however children with dyslexia may need more than this and the effects of extrinsic motivation may wear off after a time.

Ideally it is important to shift as soon as possible to intrinsic motivation. This means the child is motivated to achieve because it is important to him or her. The shift from extrinsic to intrinsic motivation is a difficult one, but one that should always be aimed for when planning learning and supporting children with dyslexia.

Social interaction can be helpful for the development of motivation as it can help develop important social skills, such as turn-taking, sharing and listening to other people's opinions. This can help to develop the child's sense of self-worth. As mentioned previously in this chapter, group dynamics can be positive or negative and it is important to ensure that the composition of the group is beneficial for the learner with dyslexia. A constructive and positive group working harmoniously can be a significant motivator. A motivated group will be able to stimulate the dyslexic learner and this can eventually lead to intrinsic motivation. The child will be doing the task because he or she wants to succeed for the sake of the group. At the same time it is important to ensure that this does not exert any pressure on the child and for that reason group work requires close monitoring.

Top Tips!

It is important to appreciate the value of group work in boosting self-esteem but also the need to carefully construct groups for optimum benefit to the child with dyslexia. He/she may feel intimidated in some groups but in others completely at ease. This can be noted through observation. It is important that information on the child is collected through observation and that this information helps to determine the composition of groups.

Motivation by feedback

Children with dyslexia need feedback to ensure they are on the correct path to obtaining results. Unfortunately feedback is often used as a means of grading or correcting work. Using feedback in this way can run the risk of de-motivating the child. It is important that feedback is seen as different from correcting work. Feedback should be continuous and formative and not necessarily come at the end of a task. Moreover feedback should be positive or framed in a positive manner. Feedback can be an important determinate of motivation and self-esteem.

Motivation by achievement

Some very successful learners with dyslexia still may not have a full appreciation of their own abilities and their own successes. They may measure or perceive success in a different way from others. There is a tendency in our society to measure one's performance against others – the foundation of our education system is based on selection. The 'must be best' syndrome is quite widespread in today's competitive society and although this has some positive elements it can be seen as a very risky strategy for children with dyslexia. It can place enormous pressure on the learner.

The key point here is 'what do we mean by achievement?' Achievement is not necessarily reaching the goal set by the teacher for the whole class. Achievement depends on the learner and their readiness for the task. If a person does not achieve then the task will need to be revised until they can achieve it! That is why the steps used in breaking down tasks are important for children with dyslexia.

The motivating environment

The environment has the potential to have a considerable impact on learning and children with dyslexia can be quite sensitive to the environment. This is an important point for teaching assistants to consider as they may have some control over the environment, particularly if they have opportunities to support children in small groups or one-to-one.

However, environmental preferences are very individual and depend a great deal on the individual's learning style. For that reason it is important for the teaching assistant to get to know the child and find out their learning and environmental preferences. For example some children with dyslexia prefer to work on their own while others prefer to work in groups. Some prefer background music while others prefer silence. Some like a lot of space while others do not mind sharing. These factors can make a real difference to the learning outcome and need to be considered when supporting children with dyslexia.

Boosting self-esteem is an individual challenge. It is important to consider the individual's needs when doing this – some strategies will have little effect while for others the same strategies can be successful.

Observing environmental and learning preferences

It is a good idea to use observation to begin with to get to know the learning and environmental preferences of the child. Before developing materials for the student it is important to obtain some knowledge of their individual preferences. One of the most effective ways of doing this is through informal observation. The headings below can be used to acquire information on children with dyslexia. For each of the headings you are asking how the learner deals with each category. For example how do they organize information? In what type of learning situations do they attend best? How do they interact with others in the class – is it a positive interaction? What type of factors motivate them to learn? The headings below can be used flexibly to obtain any type of information that can be useful. The framework is shown below (see Chapter 2 for how this can also be used in assessment):

- Organization
- Attention
- Sequencing
- Interaction
- Self-concept
- Motivation/initiative
- Independent learning.

Success through self-esteem and motivation

Other means of achieving success to develop self-esteem and motivation are as follows:

Small achievable steps

Success is an essential factor for motivation and for successful learning. If success does not result from the task then it will need to be differentiated. It is generally easier for children with dyslexia to learn new information in small steps. Many children with dyslexia are holistic learners and this means that firstly they need an overview of the topic, book or text. The key point is to ensure that each of the steps is achievable.

Progression

It is important that the child with dyslexia is able to recognize and appreciate that he/she is making some kind of progression. Some may find this difficult and progression may have to be clearly displayed for them. A framework, or even a checklist, can help the learner note his/her progression.

Checklist for Progression

Task	What I already know	What I need to find out	Progress
The effects of global warming	Climate change in some countries	What is being done to prevent it. Why it occurs	Made a list of the actions being taken by different countries. Made a list of the ways of slowing it down

Monitoring and mentoring

This can be an important role for teaching assistants. They often have access to children in an individual way and it is more possible for them to monitor the child's progress than perhaps the class teacher can. It might be useful to devise a personal checklist for teaching assistants to ensure they have considered the monitoring of self-esteem.

Personal checklist for monitoring self-esteem

1. Have I considered individual learning styles?
2. Have I ensured the task is achievable?
3. Am I aware of the different school groups, lunchtime groups and after-school groups children with dyslexia can attend? Can I do more to encourage this?
4. How do I raise the self-esteem of children with dyslexia? Can I do more to achieve this?
5. How do we cater for the children with dyslexia who are experiencing emotional difficulties?
6. How do I help dyslexic students develop motivation in the

- classroom?
- outside school?
- and at home?

7. Is there evidence in the wall displays and in the classrooms that the school is dyslexia-friendly and acknowledges the needs of children with dyslexia?

8. How do I recognize the dyslexic student's successes?

9. Do parents of children with dyslexia feel a sense of being part of the team? How are they made to feel this?

10. Am I able to show progression to the child with dyslexia – to help him or her feel they are succeeding?

Social motivation – the influence of the peer group

The peer group is very important for all children, but particularly so for children with dyslexia who may not be achieving success in the classroom. The support of the peer group can be harnessed in a number of ways. Certainly group work in the classroom is very beneficial if the group composition is carefully constructed. Out of school activities are also another way of harnessing the support and the influence of the peer group. It is important however to develop a systematic intervention programme that includes educating the class about diversity and differences. This is essentially social skills training and programmes like this are certainly not outside the remit or the capacity of the teaching assistant. Some of it can be achieved incidentally, through one-to-one or small group intervention, by listening to the child and discussing his or her views on different topics. If the topics are chosen carefully then topics such as dyslexia can be discussed in an enlightened manner and views can be discussed openly. Providing children with an opportunity to discuss topics such as dyslexia can be enriching and a learning experience for many. The result can be extremely fruitful in terms of developing a positive view of disability and differences and the spin-off effect this can have on the children with dyslexia in the school.

Chapter summary

Enhancing the self-esteem of children with dyslexia is a team effort. That is for certain. But teaching assistants can be in a privileged position by benefiting from one-to-one interaction with the dyslexic student. This can help them become aware of any child with low self-esteem and identify if that is preventing the child from developing his or her learning skills. It is also important that teaching assistants are able to communicate their observations to the class teacher and parents. This ensures that the challenge of developing self-esteem is not the responsibility of one person but is in fact a whole-school effort. This is particularly the case when one considers the role and the impact of the learning environment on the child's feelings and the subsequent effect this has on self-esteem and motivation in the classroom.

8

Working with others: the potential of teaching assistants

One of the key roles of teaching assistants is to support those around them – that includes the class teacher as well as the student. Teaching assistants are part of the school team. It is important therefore that you are able to feel part of that team. This is a management responsibility, but it is also important that teaching assistants are aware of the role of others in the school. You need experience and practice in working with others within the school. At the same time it is important for other staff in the school to be aware of the potential of teaching assistants and that they are able to include them in all aspects of school work.

This chapter will therefore focus on the following:

1. The potential of teaching assistants
2. Training needs
3. Working with children
4. Working with teachers
5. Curriculum support.

The potential of teaching assistants

Many countries now have well-developed training programmes for teaching assistants. It is widely accepted that teaching assistants need training and that their skills should be maximized and developed more than has been the case previously. As indicated earlier in this book you are in a prime position to establish close connections with students and to offer valuable support to teachers. The degree of this support can vary depending on the level of training and the nature of the employment contract offered. Again this can vary from country to country.

In the UK the government have established a basis for different levels of teaching assistants. When one looks at the remit for Level 4 Teaching Assistant one can readily note the considerable potential they have for playing an important role in the school and additionally carving out a useful career path for themselves. This type of initiative is necessary if teaching assistants are to obtain not only job satisfaction, but in many situations, establish themselves as key members of school staff.

In terms of supporting students and delivering learning programmes, the UK government proposed that Level Four Teaching Assistants should complement the professional work

Reflect on your role in the classroom and in the school. How can your classroom remit be extended to support others within the school? Can this be done through dissemination of information on resources to other staff, or through communication with other teachers on student's progress. It is important to appreciate that although your role may be primarily classroom based it is possible to usefully extend that role to supporting other teachers and to become a school resource. This of course has time management implications and to implement this perspective the school management needs to be understanding and supportive.

of teachers by taking responsibility for learning activities which may involve planning, preparing and delivering activities for individuals or groups, or for whole classes. Additionally it is suggested they should also be involved in the monitoring, assessing, recording and reporting on pupils' achievement, progress and development. This in itself envisages a key role for teaching assistants not only for one or two students but within the whole school.

A similar perspective can be seen in Canada. For example the guide for teaching assistants training at University of British Columbia (UBC), Okanagan, suggests that teaching assistants should be seen as facilitators of learning and the aim is that they are able to enhance student's ability to achieve. The guide also states that teaching assistants should demonstrate leadership in the classroom, provide motivation for learners and contribute positively to the learning process of students. This includes monitoring student progress, allowing students input into decisions, assessment, choices and giving positive feedback.

Similar to the role of Level Four Teaching Assistants in the UK, the UBC Okanagan guide assumes a similar role for the teaching assistants they train. Many of the points they make refer to issues relating to good teaching and those features would be an integral component of a regular teacher training course. For example the guide provides questions to consider when planning for a lesson. These include:

- What are the students to learn and why?
- What do the students already know?
- What is the most appropriate delivery technique to convey the information?
- What is the most logical sequence to pursue?
- How will you know if the desired learning has taken place?

(Source: UBC Okanagan, *A Guide for Effective Practices for Teaching Assistants*, Fall 2006, page 27.)

Although the guide was not written specifically for those teaching dyslexic students, many of the suggestions are in fact dyslexia-friendly. For example the guide suggests the following:

- Overheads should not be cluttered.
- Information should be presented in small chunks with opportunities for the student to take breaks.
- Transitions from one area of learning to another are carefully planned.
- There is an awareness of time management and students' needs in relation to this.
- Begin with a visual aid/story.
- Liberally use metaphors, analogies, vivid images and anecdotes.

There is certainly a significant effort made to ensure that whatever type of situation teaching assistants find themselves in they will be able to cope with it. The guide also provides suggestions on direct instruction such as:

- Debates
- Role playing
- Brainstorming
- Cooperative learning groups for reading
- Problem-solving learning.

There is also guidance on independent study (indirect instruction), such as:

- Reports – reading for meaning
- Learning activity packages
- Reflective discussion
- Learning contracts
- Concept mapping.

Additionally the guide underlines the disparity in both the training and the role of classroom assistants, but without doubt it highlights the potential of teaching assistants for playing a key role in the school.

The debate

Interestingly enough, in the UK the BBC featured a debate on the role of teaching assistants (www.news.bbc.co.uk/go/pr/fr/-/1/hi/talking_point/2965983.stm) essentially asking what role teaching assistants should be expected to undertake? This debate stemmed from trade union pressure that government proposals to allow teaching assistants to take charge of classes was both unwise and unjust. Furthermore there was a view that this would result in reductions in the number of trained teachers in the classroom as teachers would be replaced by the cheaper option – teaching assistants. They put the question to listeners and it is interesting to study a sample of the responses. Some of the comments to the question, which was 'should teaching assistants be allowed to teach without supervision?' include the following: 'In my view this is equivalent to asking a flight attendant to replace an airline pilot on difficult landings – shouldn't the "problem" children get the "professional"?'; 'Classroom assistants should never replace teachers but they do have a very vital role to play in education'; and 'I worked as a supply teacher and I could not be more grateful for the teaching assistants that helped me and assisted me with the control of the class and the work. I think they are as valuable members of staff as teachers and they do a good job.' There was also a very telling comment from a qualified teacher who only wants to work as a teaching assistant. The respondent suggested 'that there are many others in this situation who prefer to work as classroom assistants and that classroom assistants can have a positive effect on education in this country. I've seen many teachers whose control of the class left a lot to be desired and many classroom assistants who would have put the teacher to shame'.

It appears these respondents have identified some of the key aspects of the debate – that is, teaching assistants need comprehensive and quality training and furthermore, with training they have considerable potential to play a key role in the school.

Reflect on the issues you come across in carrying out your daily job. How can these issues be resolved? Try developing a chart with the issues, the impact, how these can be resolved, and the action needed to try to resolve these (see the chart below).

Fulfilling potential

Issue	Impact on role	How can it be resolved?	Action/results
Being asked to photocopy most of day	Have not got time to prepare for students	Discussion with head teacher	
Need more information on dyslexia	Not clear about how to approach the different types of difficulties dyslexic children may have	Discussion with class teacher, training course on dyslexia, discussion with other teaching assistants in other schools	

Been on a course for circle time and now want to implement it in the class	Frustrating if you have been on a course and cannot follow it through in the class	Discussion with the teacher before going on a course to ensure that it can be implemented	Jointly with the teacher work out the circle time activities that can best fit into the school and the class
I seem to be the parents' main contact, how can I be sure I am relaying the correct information to parents?	This is very important and can result in inconsistent information being relayed to parents	Keep a log of the information given to parents and discuss this with the teacher. Similarly the teacher should do this too to ensure consistency	This has implications for consultation time with the teacher

Fitting into the school

There are a number of issues that need to be considered in relation to teaching assistants being part of the school. Many of these issues can have an impact on the whole school and the teaching staff. It is important that the school management are involved and aware of the nature of these issues and that they ensure that teaching assistants are involved in every aspect of the school.

One of the key issues is that of professional development. It is only through professional development that teaching assistants can obtain recognition and status within the school. In the light of the growing responsibility being given to teaching assistants the question of training has become increasingly important.

Pathways for training

Although teaching assistants require a generic course in teaching and learning in order to provide a basis for their classroom work, it is also important that they are offered specific, individually tailored courses to meet the variety of situations they come across in schools. Often the actual workload of a teaching assistant can vary from school to school so therefore the role of teaching assistants can vary depending on the school. This has training implications, as some teaching assistants may need different types of courses from others. For that reason they need a generic core course and a number of optional specialized types of courses depending on the actual nature of the work they are involved in. Some of these specialized courses could include:

- teaching skills needed for teaching reading, spelling and mathematics
- dealing with parents
- social and emotional aspects of learning such as circle time and dealing with stress in students
- working with ICT
- study skills
- learning styles
- differentiation
- evaluating resources.

The core courses should include:

- working with others
- understanding the reading process
- helping with spelling
- dealing with mathematics
- writing skills.

Training is important for teaching assistants and the availability of specific courses for teaching assistants is becoming more widespread. It is important that teaching assistants also recognize this need as well as the school management. This will provide the opportunity for a more professional and more widely accepted role for teaching assistants.

Support for pupils

Supporting children will always be the key role for teaching assistants, particularly supporting students with specific requirements such as students with dyslexia. Some suggestions for support are shown below:

- It is important to establish effective working relationships with pupils. This involves getting to know the pupil through one-to-one contact and finding out his or her learning preferences, identifying any areas of concern such as their self-esteem.
- Develop and implement individual programmes. The starting point for this is your knowledge of the pupil. This information can also be obtained through observation as well as one-to-one interaction. Then the teaching assistant should discuss the pupil's curriculum needs with the class teacher and work out priority areas. The development of the IEP should be a joint venture as should its monitoring and the review. It is important to identify short- and long-term plans when developing an IEP as well as gathering information on resources that can support the IEP.
- Ensure as far as possible the inclusion and acceptance of all pupils within the classroom. Even if the teaching

assistant has been nominated to deal with one or two students it is important to be aware of the needs of the whole class.

■ Teaching assistants should try to obtain a balance between offering support to students in the whole class or group context and at the same time appreciate student's individual needs. It is important to offer consistent support to all pupils whilst recognizing and responding to their individual needs. This can be a difficult balancing act but it is important not to single out an individual pupil all the time.

■ Try to facilitate cooperative and group work as this can be good for students' self-esteem, but you need to ensure that the group dynamics are positive and constructive for the student with dyslexia.

■ It is important to try to encourage independence by helping the student become an independent learner. This is an important point as it is too easy for students who have access to a teaching assistant to become dependent on them. Students need to be weaned off this dependence and they need to be encouraged to take responsibility for their own learning.

■ Feedback, recognition and reward – these elements are important for students to progress and to believe in their own abilities. They need feedback constantly and achievements should be recognized. It is important to appreciate that an achievement for students with dyslexia can be different from that of other students – it is important to acknowledge their strengths as well, and feed back this information to the student.

Support for teachers

Some suggestions for support for teachers that can be offered by teaching assistants include:

■ Organizing and managing the resources – it is important that this is not seen as the main job of teaching assistants.

At the same time they can be in a good position to become familiar with a range of resources and use this knowledge to benefit other teachers in the school.

- Jointly plan teaching and learning objectives – this is important particularly if the teaching is going to be implemented by teaching assistants, it will be beneficial if they are involved in the planning and re-evaluation of the programmes of work.

- Assist in the re-evaluation of lesson plans and IEPs – this will ensure that the knowledge teaching assistants gain from working closely with a child can be used to its maximum benefit through extended consultations with the teacher.

- Reporting on student's progress. It is important also that teaching assistants are able to contribute to the monitoring and reporting process in place in the school. They will be aware of students' achievements and will be able to provide information on that in the development of progress reports.

- Teaching assistants can have responsibility for working independently with students. This means they need to exert a degree of control and authority over students and therefore need to have training in behaviour management techniques. It is important that the class teacher and the teaching assistant work collaboratively and consistently over discipline and control.

- Working collaboratively with parents – teaching assistants may be in a better position to see parents more regularly than teachers, especially if they are working with children in the early years. Again it is important that a consistent message is conveyed to parents and this again means that teaching assistants and classroom teachers must work closely and keep the other informed of any information that has been passed to parents.

- Preparing worksheets – teaching assistants can take a great deal of pressure off teachers by assisting in the preparation of worksheets. It is important that these are prepared in a dyslexia-friendly manner. It might be a good idea to develop a checklist after making up a worksheet to ensure it is dyslexia-friendly. The checklist could include the following:

- Are there multisensory activities?
- Is the pace of work differentiated to accommodate differences in processing speed?
- Is the assessment of learning outcomes varied so that investigative and experiential assessment is considered?
- Are learning styles being taken into account?
- Are the worksheets in large type and well spaced with visuals and short sentences? The visual presentation of worksheets is crucially important as a motivating factor for students with dyslexia.
- Is non-white paper being used in order to ensure that there is no visual distortion when reading print?
- Are there opportunities for work to be presented on a word processor?
- Does the worksheet begin with an overview of the topic?
- Are there opportunities to allow students to reflect on their learning?

Curriculum support

- Has the potential for ICT been acknowledged?
- Has the student's cultural and language background been taken into account?
- Have any specialized materials and resources been sought (see appendices for resources)?
- Have the curriculum objectives been discussed with the teacher?

Support for the school

As indicated earlier it is important that teaching assistants are viewed as a school resource and not earmarked only for a specific child. It is appropriate therefore that they become familiar with school policies and practices. This includes:

- an understanding of health and safety issues
- knowledge of legislation on data protection
- being aware of the school ethos and vision
- being aware of the role of visiting professionals and specialists
- collaborating with other teaching assistants in the school.

While it is important to appreciate that teaching assistants should not take over the role of the teacher, it is also important to ensure that their potential is used to its maximum. This will provide opportunities to enhance the professionalism of teaching assistants. This is important otherwise they may be misused and consequently become frustrated and left with less job satisfaction than they may otherwise have if they were able to play a more prominent role in the classroom and in the school.

Chapter summary

This chapter has provided some suggestions and frameworks to support the professional development of teaching assistants. We have suggested that teaching assistants have considerable potential to offer support to staff and to become a major contributor within the school. One of the key features of this is the commitment to training and the acceptance of the potential of teaching assistants who have higher levels of training. In the case of students with dyslexia it is critically important that teaching assistants have at least some training on dyslexia. The same would apply to other learning disabilities such as dyspraxia and dyscalculia. This chapter has provided some indication of the different areas of support that teaching assistants can contribute towards. In order for this to become a reality however there needs to be a firm commitment from management to recognize the potential of teaching assistants and to invest in their training. The key however to an effective role for teaching assistants within the school environment is the collaborative spirit that prevails between teachers and teaching assistants. Collaboration is essential and both teachers and teaching assistants have an important role to play in developing a collaborative ethos within the school.

Glossary

ADHD – children with ADHD (Attention Deficit Hyperactivity Disorder) will have a short attention span and tend to work on a number of different tasks at the same time. They will be easily distracted and may have difficulty settling in some classrooms, particularly if there are a number of competing distractions. It is also possible for some children to have attention difficulties without hyperactivity (this is referred to as ADD).

Auditory discrimination – many children with dyslexia can have difficulties with auditory discrimination. This refers to the difficulties in identifying specific sounds and in distinguishing these sounds from other similar sounds. This can be associated with the phonological difficulties experienced by children with dyslexia (see **phonological difficulties**). Hearing loss or partial and intermittent hearing loss can also be associated with auditory discrimination.

Bottom-up – this refers to the method of reading that uses decoding skills, therefore reading accuracy is crucial. It means that the reader has to have a good grasp of letters and the sounds, and be able to blend these together to make words. Some readers with dyslexia may confuse words with similar sounds or those that look visually similar. It is common for beginning readers to learn to read this way. It is essential that children with dyslexia are taught through the bottom-up process in order to ensure they are familiar with the basic sounds and sound combinations (for comparison see **top-down**).

Cognitive – this refers to the learning and thinking process. It is the process that describes how learners take in information and how they retain and understand information.

Decoding – this refers to reading processing and specifically to the breaking down of words into the individual sounds.

Differentiation – this is the process of adapting materials and teaching to suit a range of learners' abilities and level of attainment. Usually differentiation refers to the task, the teaching, the resources and the assessment. Each of these areas can be differentiated to suit the needs of individual or groups of learners.

Dyscalculia – this describes children and adults who have difficulties with numeracy. This could be due to difficulties with the computation of numbers, remembering numbers or reading the instructions associated with number problems.

Dysgraphia – this describes difficulties with handwriting. Some dyspraxic and dyslexic children may also show signs of dysgraphia. Children with dysgraphia will benefit from lined paper as they have visual/spatial problems and they may have an awkward pencil grip.

Dyslexia – refers to difficulties in accessing print but also other factors such as memory, processing speed, sequencing, directions, syntax, spelling and written work can also be challenging. Children with dyslexia often have phonological difficulties which results in poor word attack skills. In many cases they require a dedicated one-to-one intervention programme.

Dyspraxia – this refers to children and adults with coordination difficulties. It can also be described as Developmental Co-ordination Disorder (DCD).

Eye tracking – this is the skill of being able to read a line and keep the eyes on track throughout the line. Children with poor eye tracking may omit lines or words on a page. Sometimes masking a part of a line or page, or using a ruler can help with eye tracking.

Information processing – this is a process that describes how children and adults learn new information. It is usually described as a cycle – input, cognition and output. Often children with dyslexia can have difficulties at all the stages of information processing and dyslexia can be referred to as a difficulty or a difference in information processing.

Learning disabilities – this is a general term to describe the range of specific learning difficulties such as dyslexia, dyspraxia, dyscalculia and dysgraphia. Often referred to as LD it is not related to low intelligence and children with LD are usually in the average to above average intelligence range.

Learning styles – this can describe the learner's preferences for learning – these can be for using visual, auditory, kinesthetic or tactile stimuli but it can also relate to environmental preferences such as sound, the use of music when learning, preferences for time of day and working in pairs, groups or individually. There is a lot of literature on learning styles but it is still seen as quite controversial very likely because there are hundreds of different instruments all of which claim to measure learning styles. Many learners are in fact quite adaptable and can adapt to different types of learning situations and environments. Nevertheless it is a useful concept to apply in the classroom, particularly for children with learning disabilities as using learning styles it is easier to identify their strengths and use these in preparing materials and in teaching.

Long-term memory – this is used to recall information that has been learned and needs to be recalled for a purpose. Many children with dyslexia can have difficulty with long-term memory as they have not organized the information they have learned, and recalling it can be challenging as they may not have enough cues to assist with recall. Study skills programmes can help with long-term memory.

Metacognition – this is the process of thinking about thinking, that is being aware of how one learns and how a problem was solved. It is a process-focussed approach and one that is necessary for effective and efficient learning. Many children with dyslexia may have poor metacognitive awareness because they are unsure of the process of learning. For that reason study skills programmes can be useful.

Multiple intelligences – first developed by Howard Gardner in the early 1980s in his book *Frames of Mind* it turns conventional views of intelligence on its head. Gardner provides insights into the eight intelligences and shows how the educational and the social and emotional needs of all children can be catered for through the use of these intelligences. Traditionally intelligence has been equated with school success, but often this focuses predominantly on the verbal and language aspects of performance. Gardner's model is broader than that, which indicates that the traditional view of intelligence may be restrictive (see Chapter 7).

Multisensory – this refers to the use of a range of modalities in learning. In this context multisensory usually refers to the use of visual, auditory, kinesthetic and tactile learning. It is generally accepted that children with dyslexia need a multisensory approach that utilizes all of these modalities.

Neurological – this refers to brain associated factors (or brain structures), that is the different components of the brain, or brain processing, and how the components interact with each other. The research in dyslexia shows that both brain structure and brain processing factors are implicated in dyslexia.

Peer tutoring – this is when two or more children work together and try to learn from each other. It may also be the case that an older, more proficient learner is working with a younger, less accomplished learner and the younger one is the tutee and the older student the tutor.

Phonological awareness – this refers to the process of becoming familiar with the letter sounds and letter combinations that make the sounds in reading print. There are 44 sounds in the English language and some sounds are very similar. This can be confusing and challenging for children with dyslexia and they often get the sounds confused or have difficulty in retaining and recognizing them when reading or speaking.

Specific learning difficulties – this refers to the range of difficulties experienced by students that can be of a specific nature such as reading, coordination, spelling or handwriting. There are quite a number of specific learning difficulties and they can be seen as being distinct from general learning difficulties. In the latter case, children with general learning difficulties usually find most areas of the curriculum challenging and may have a lower level of comprehension than children with specific learning difficulties.

Top-down – this refers to the reading process and particularly the procedure and strategies used by young readers. The top-down method means that the reader begins with the context and the background of the text and uses contextual cues to help with the reading process. In the top-down model, reading for meaning is more important than reading accuracy. Language experience is an important prerequisite for reading using the top-down method (see **bottom-up** for comparison).

Working memory – this is the first stage in short-term memory. It involves the learner holding information in short-term store and carrying out a processing activity simultaneously. Working memory is when one or more stimuli are held in the memory for a short period of time. Children with dyslexia often experience difficulties with working memory as they have problems holding a number of different pieces of information at the same time. It is important they receive one piece of information at a time.

Appendix 1
Identifying learning styles

This is a shortened form of a learning styles questionnaire (Reid 2007) and it may be useful if you want to obtain some idea of a student's learning style.

1. Do you prefer to work when it is quiet or with background noise?
2. Do you like to talk with people while you are working or work quietly by yourself?
3. Do you like to listen to music while you are working?
4. Do you prefer to work with a dim table light or bright lights?
5. Do you like to work with a jacket or fleece on or do you prefer a t-shirt or something cool?
6. Do you like a lot of space in the classroom?
7. Do you like to have your own desk and work space or are you happy sharing this with someone else?
8. Do you prefer learning visually?
9. Do you prefer learning through listening to someone?
10. Do you like to make or do something when you are learning?
11. Do you like to move around when you are working on something?
12. Do you prefer to take time to think about something before doing it or do you want to do it straight away?

Using the results

It is important to discuss the results with the student. Discuss what the results may mean to the student's study patterns and show how they might be able to incorporate their responses into their classwork and independent study. This is an important part of the exercise. The implications of most of the responses to the questions are self-explanatory and it is important to help the student work out how they use these responses in their learning plan. The last question, 12, may be less obvious – it indicates whether the student has a reflective or an impulsive style. If he or she takes time to think before acting on something this would indicate a reflective style of learning and additional time should be allocated for this reflection. If they have an impulsive style then some type of self-monitoring or teacher monitoring needs to be built into the student's learning programme.

(From Reid, G. (2007) *Motivating Learners in the Classroom: Ideas and Strategies*. London: Sage.)

Appendix 2
Games and activities –
and where to get them

Crossbow Education (www.crossboweducation.com)

Magic E spin-it: ages six +

A popular resource for learning and reinforcing the 'magic e' spelling rule. Five graded boards enable students to 'try out' magic e spellings on a selection of real words and non-words. Does it spell a word, or doesn't it? And was it a word to start with? Vocabulary and word-recognition skills are valuable extras to the main benefit of this game, which can be used for both initial teaching and reinforcement purposes. Boards are graded according to spelling difficulty, starting with three-letter a, i, o words on board one and ending with bath/bathe, ph and silent k words etc. on board five. 2–4 players per spinner board can play, which means that one pack could resource over half of a mixed-ability top infants class!

Knockout: ages eight +

This comprehensive resource provides 24 suits of vowel digraph spelling patterns, with eight cards to each suit. The game format is whist – knockout whist, or 'trumps' – which involves the principle of 'following suit' to collect the highest number of 'tricks' (sets of cards). Players must read aloud the words they play. They **see** the suit, **hear** the vowel sound and **identify** the spelling pattern with its family as they **physically play** the card. Four suits at a time are used (as in ordinary playing cards), and each suit is changed once success has been achieved with it. A diagnostic checklist for short-term and long-term memory is provided with the rules, to be photocopied for each student.

Vowel digraph triplets: ages six +
This contains 21 vowel digraph suits in sets of three, with one rhyming pair and one non-rhyming pair for each medial vowel digraph. A variety of games can be played for phonics and auditory discrimination. Ideal for work with younger children, but also suitable for older students still working at this level.

18 phonic games from dyslexia teaching pioneer Prof. Beve Hornsby, linking with Stage One of Alpha to Omega (Hornsby and Shear 1980).

1. 'Count the Beat' - Syllable pairs game.
2. 'Top Gun' – Short vowel pairs games.
3 'Snail Slide' – Consonant blends - 's' blends.
4. 'Crackers' – Consonant blends - 'r' blends.
5. 'Glue Up the Blanket' – Consonant blends – 'l' blends.
6. 'Three Square Squirrels' –Triple blends pairs.
7. 'Ants Unch at the End' – Assimilation pairs.
8. 'Ed's dotted game' – 'ed' pairs game.
9. 'King Fang's Drink' – 'ng' and 'nk' pairs game.
10. 'Shark or Spider' – 'ar', 'or' and 'er' pairs game.
11. 'Muff And Scarf' – Flossy words, 'ff' or 'f'.
12. 'Gulls Goal' – Flossy words, 'll' or 'l'.
13. 'Duck Park' – Flossy words, 'ck' or 'k'.
14. 'Pete's Magic 'e'" – Pairs game.
15. 'Double Trouble' – Suffixing game.
16. 'Drop the Shake' – Suffixing magic 'e'.
17. 'Wining or Winning' – Suffixing game.
18. 'Playing Boy or Dutiful City' – Suffixing game.

Smart Kids (www.smartkids.co.uk)

Let's Spell (end with a blend): ages five to six
This range of flipbooks covers CVC, CCVC, CVCC and CVVC spelling patterns. The design provides students with a fun way to experiment with many letter combinations as they assemble words, and offers early readers a hands-on approach for developing spelling skills. There are five books in the *Let's Spell* series, each with a self-correcting word list at the back.

Smart Chute
This high-quality card flipper is a fun way to develop key numeracy skills. When posting the card in the Smart Chute, the student can say the answer (such as the equation $5 + 3 = ?$) and the correct answer then miraculously appears at the bottom. The Smart Chute is a very popular resource and children will be intrigued as to how the Smart Chute can work out the correct answer. It reinforces key concepts and develops memory skills. The Smart Chute comes in three plastic pieces, which clip together and can be dismantled easily for portability. The Chute itself is made out of solid plastic and its durability will withstand maximum classroom use. There are over 40 literacy and numeracy cards compatible with the Smart Chute, plus a set of blank cards so that teachers can make their own packs.

Rhyme magnets
Each colour-coded magnetic tile has a familiar picture which matches a corresponding sound. Students sort the picture with the sound onto a magnetic board. The pack contains 65 different tiles.

Blank Game Board (see Chapter 3)
This game board is referred to in Chapter 3. A blank game board can be used to create a game that reinforces exactly what you are teaching. You can write vocabulary words on it,

spelling concepts, spelling rules, penmanship formations to practise, reading comprehension questions or anything else you can think of. Just think up questions to support what the student is learning, write them on the game board and then laminate it or put it in a page protector so it will last longer. Try making your own dice out of a wooden cube using only the numbers 1 and 2. That way they will land on more questions and the game will last longer. Or use a spinner with 1, 2 and 3. When you pull out a game to play many students actually forget they are learning. We find if you just write the concepts on a game board and give them a dice or a spinner, suddenly they are happy and their tutor (or TA) is 'the best'.

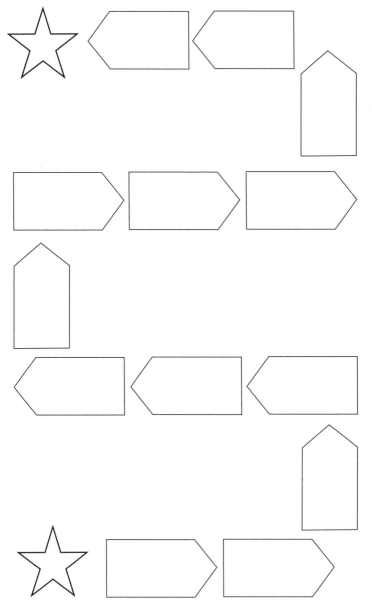

Blank game board

Appendix 3
The use of ICT in the classroom

There is a wealth of information on the pros and cons of using ICT in schools. See TeacherNet's information on ICT in schools (www.teachernet.gov.uk) and also the book by Jane Healy, *Failure to connect: how computers affect our children's minds and what we can do about it* (1998).

The website www.dyslexic.com/readingpen has a range of resources for ICT in the classroom specifically designed for dyslexic learners. These include:

■ **The Reading Pen –** this scans, displays, reads aloud and defines words. Designed specifically for people with dyslexia who require support with reading, the Reading Pen is an ideal tool to help with reading.
■ **AcceleRead, AcceleWrite CD-Rom with cards –** is a teaching guide on how to use speech technology to improve literacy skills. AcceleRead, AcceleWrite by Vivienne Clifford and Martin Miles provides full instructions on how to use almost any computer to improve reading and writing skills. The detailed electronic manual explains how reading and writing can be improved dramatically using computer text-to-speech software plus a clear explanation of the theory behind the approach. The comprehensive package also includes perforated, colour-coded flash cards, photocopiable record sheets, along with blank flash cards for you to

print off with your own sentences. Requires a computer that has a sound card, and a talking word processor or text-to-speech program.

■ **Read & Write Standard, published by Texthelp** – Read &Write offers users speech feedback and word prediction for practically any Windows program. Read & Write has been specifically designed for users with dyslexia and provides many tools to help access and compose written material. Features include high-quality speech feedback, phonetic spell checker, word prediction, dictionary and talking calculator. The Teacher's Toolkit enables teachers, administrators or parents to customize Read and Write to meet the requirements of the individual; including turning on or off functions (such as the spell checker during exams) and monitoring spelling mistakes and usage logs. The style of the toolbar can be customized to be appropriate to the age of the user. Users can chose whether they want basic or advanced word lists and definitions in the dictionary, word prediction list and homophone checker. Features:

– Extensive speech feedback functions using the highest quality voices available. Speech feedback options allow you to hear text as you type letter-by-letter, word-by-word or sentence-by-sentence or have text highlighted as it is read out.

– Synchronized speech with text highlighted within an application, in a separate windows or with one word displayed at a time.

– Screen-reading options enable speech from icons, menus, help files and menus.

– Spell checking as you type or by marked block. The spell checker includes medical and scientific words as well as town and city names.

– Homophone support including highlighting confusable words within Word documents.

- Phonetic spell checking gives Spelled Alike and Sounds Alike suggestions.
- Word suggestion and completion ('word prediction') for slow typists based on sentence context and specialist dictionaries.
- Spoken selection lists for spelling, prediction and dictionary.
- Simple calculator with in-built speech functions.
- Speaking Help file.
- Teacher's Toolkit and user-specific settings for use with multiple users.
- Abbreviation expansion.
- Automatic word endings.
- Extensive, speech-enabled dictionary with a choice of basic or advanced definitions.
- Word Wizard word finder that combines dictionary and thesaurus to help when you are lost for words.

www.dyslexic.com also has the following software available:

- Assessment software: software such as Lexion and the Lucid range for assessing verbal and non-verbal skills and indicating the likelihood of dyslexia; also programs to simulate the experience of being dyslexic and to detect disabilities within a group of employees.
- Cross-curricular software: dyslexia-friendly software for use across the curriculum.
- General and student software: standard office and productivity applications as well as more advanced graphic design and multimedia software. This category includes student editions of these packages.
- Numeracy software: basic mathematics, fractions, telling the time or calculating money and includes the popular Numbershark.
- Organizational software: concept-mapping and Mind-

Mapping software to help you get ideas down and organize them, useful for those with dyslexia.

▨ Reading and literacy software and tools: a range of tools and software to help overcome literacy problems, such as dyslexia, and visual impairment. This includes text-to-speech tools and also scanning and OCR software, so you can have electronic versions of paper documents.

▨ Speech recognition software: assistive technology (including market-leader Dragon) that displays your dictation on the screen and saves it in electronic format. Spell check and editing facilities give you full control over the text. Mathematics and science versions also available.

▨ Spelling and writing software: software to help with everything from spelling, grammar, punctuation and typing to actually shaping and producing written work.

Other suppliers include:

www.cricksoft.com/uk – they have created many high-quality resources for use with Clicker 5, a talking word processor – you can write by using the keyboard, or by selecting letters, words or phrases in the Clicker Grid.

xavier.bangor.ac.uk/xavier/sounds_rhymes.shtml – have a very comprehensive range of software for dyslexic pupils. One example is:

Sounds & Rhymes v2: Over 16 different learning activities

▨ Skills taught range from vowel sounds to consonant blends
▨ Practise a single rule or any combination
▨ Simple to set up and use
▨ Easily track the progress of pupils.

Starting with single sounds and culminating in the identification of rhyming words, a progression of tasks aims to develop recognition of short vowels and automatic response to sounds within words.

The Sounds task concentrates on the standard five vowel sounds, presenting several practice formats varied between the pupils listening to the initial sound of a word and matching it to a vowel or grouping simple three-letter words by their middle letter.

The Rhymes task covers many topics – initial and final consonant, word endings, rhyming words, matching words, odd word out and others. Each of the tasks can be practised with or without the aid of textual clues, making the task purely auditory if required.

With this latest incarnation of the program a new feature has been added. The program can now also be used to help students with consonant blends, with the ability to choose from initial blends (**fr**og), final blends (pa**st**) or both (**spr**a**ng**).

(See also www.gavinreid.co.uk under links for full range of stockists and publishers of dyslexia appropriate materials.)

Appendix 4
Websites and contacts

Dyslexia resources

Crossbow Education, 41 Sawpit Lane, Brocton, Stafford, ST17 0TE.
www.crossboweducation.com

IANSYT Ltd, The White House, 72 Fen Road, Cambridge, CB4 1UN.
www.iansyst.co.uk and www.dyslexic.co.uk

Xavier Educational Software Ltd, School of Psychology, University of Wales, Bangor, Gwynedd, LL57 2AS.
www.xavier.bangor.ac.uk

Texthelp Systems Ltd, Enkalon Business Centre, 25 Randalstown Road, Antrim BT41 4LJ, Northern Ireland.
www.texthelp.com

LDA – Literacy Resources for Special Needs
www.LDAlearning.com

The Lind Institute
www.lind-institute.com

Learning Works International Ltd, 9 Barrow Close, Marlborough, Wiltshire SN8 2BD.

www.learning-works.org.uk
Provides a range of materials for children to enhance learning. Some excellent materials and activities on memory work. They also publish an excellent book on dyscalculia by Anne Henderson, Fil Came and Mel Brough (see references).

Audio books
www.simplyaudiobooks.ca
www.school.booksontape.com
www.kidsbooksandpuppets.com

The Mystery of the Lost Letters
www.ditt-online.org
A tri-lingual, self-help tool for dyslexic learners and their mentors.

Information and support

REACH Learning Center 121A–123 East 15th Street, North Vancouver, BC Canada V7M 1R7.
www.reachlearningcenter.com

Red Rose School, St Annes on Sea, Lancashire FY8 2NQ – provides for the educational, emotional and social needs of no greater than 48 boys and girls, aged between seven and 16 years.
www.redroseschool.co.uk

Dr Gavin Reid – Psychologist, Reach Learning Center, BC, Canada; Director, Red Rose School, UK; Consultant, Centre for Child Evaluation and Teaching (CCET) Kuwait; Trainer, Learning Works International.
www.gavinreid.co.uk, reid@reachlearningcenter.com

The International Dyslexia Association (formerly the Orton Dyslexia Association). Provides resources for professionals

and families dealing with individuals with reading disabilities.
www.interdys.org

British Dyslexia Association (BDA) – Information and advice
on dyslexia for dyslexic people and those who support them.
www.bdadyslexia.org.uk

Learning Works International runs accredited courses,
produces materials, books and other educational products.
www.learning-works.org.uk

Creative Learning Company, New Zealand
www.creativelearningcentre.com

Canada Dyslexia Association, 290 Picton Avenue, Ottawa,
Ontario.
cda@ottawa.com and www.dyslexiaassociation.ca

Dyslexia Parents Resource
www.dyslexia-parent.com

Family Onwards
www.familyonwards.com

www.TheSchoolDaily.com, 5 Durham Street, Box 8577,
Christchurch, New Zealand provides a wealth of useful and
up-to-date information on education and dyslexia.

Dyslexia Teacher – for teachers of children and students with
dyslexia. Provides information on teaching methods, recognizing dyslexia, assessment, books, news, research and teachers'
contributions.
www.dyslexia-teacher.com

Learning Disabilities Worldwide – causes, diagnoses, treat-
ment, early signs and warnings.
www.LDWorldwide.org

Dyslexia Institute is now known as Dyslexia Action provides information about dyslexia services. Dyslexia associated training, teaching and publication details. Local UK groups.
www.dyslexia-inst.org.uk/

The Dyslexia Parents Resource – free information about dyslexia and dyslexia testing, free dyslexia magazine for parents, a free dyslexia advice line.
www.dyslexia-parent.com

Dyslexia Association of Ireland
www.dyslexia.ie/dysexp.htm

Adult Dyslexia Organization – the Adult Dyslexia Organization (ADO) provides help and assistance to all dyslexic adults.
www.futurenet.co.uk/charity/ado/index.html

Scoop: Dyslexia Foundation celebrating Ministry of Education recognition of dyslexia.
www.scoop.co.nz/stories/ED0704/S00074.htm

European Dyslexia Association/Dyspel
www.dyspel.org/eda

Fun Track Learning Center, PO Box 134, Mosman Park, WA 6912
info@funtrack.com.au, www.funtrack.com.au

Dr Loretta Giorcelli – Giorcelli Educational Consultancy Services
http://www.doctorg.org/

Other specific learning difficulties

SNAP Assessment
A tool to inform about 17 specific learning difficulties, SNAP-SpLD is comprehensive, structured and systematic: it maps

each child's own mix of problems onto an overall matrix of learning, social and personal difficulties.
www.snapassessment.com/

Attention deficit disorders

The National Attention Deficit Disorder Information Service
www.addiss.co.uk

Attention Deficit Disorder Association
www.chadd.org and www.add.org

ADHD behaviour management
www.StressFreeADHD.com

ADHD books
www.adders.org and www.addwarehouse.com

ADHD diet
www.feingold.org

Dyscovery Centre – multidisciplinary assessment centre for dyslexia, dyspraxia, attention deficit disorders, and autistic spectrum disorders.
www.dyscovery.co.uk

Developmental Coordination Disorders/Dyspraxia

Dyspraxia Foundation
www.dyspraxiafoundation.org.uk

Dyspraxia Connexion – website offers support, information and practical help.
www.dysf.fsnet.co.uk

QuEST therapies
www.questtherapies.com

www.hiddenhandicap.co.uk

www.dyspraxia.org.nz

Mindroom – charity aimed at helping children and adults with learning difficulties.
www.mindroom.org

Autistic Spectrum Disorders and Asperger's Syndrome

National Autistic Society
www.nas.org.uk

www.futurehorizons-autism.com

Speech and language difficulties

Afasic
www.afasic.org.uk

I CAN
www.ican.org.uk
www.childspeech.net

www.talkingpoint.org.uk

References

Buzan, T. (2003) *Mind Maps for Kids: An Introduction*. London: HarperCollins.

Chinn, S. (2002) 'Learning Styles and Maths'. Paper presented at OSL Teachers Conference, Greenwich, London 12 October 2002.

Chinn, S. (2004) *The Trouble with Maths*. London: Routledge.

Cline, T. (2000) 'Multilingualism and dyslexia: challenges for research and practice' in *Dyslexia*, 6:1, 3–12.

Eadon, H. (2005) *Dyslexia and Drama*. London: David Fulton.

Gardner, H. (1983) *Frames of Mind: The Theory of Multiple Intelligences*. New York: Harper and Row.

Healy, J. (1998) *Failure to connect: how computers affect our children's minds and what we can do about it*. New York: Touchstone Books.

Henderson, A., Brough, M. and Came, F. (2003) *Working with Dyscalculia: Recognising Dyscalculia and Overcoming Barriers to Learning in Maths*. Marlborough: Learning Works International.

Hornsby, B. and Shear, F. (1980) *Alpha to Omega: The A-Z of teaching reading, writing and spelling*. London: Heinemann Educational.

Ofsted (2002) *Teaching assistants in primary schools: an evaluation of the quality and impact of their work* (reference HMI 434), viewed 30 July 2007 (www.ofsted.gov.uk).

Portwood, M. (2004) *Dyslexia and Physical Education*. London: David Fulton.

Reid, G. (2007) *Motivating Learners in the Classroom: Ideas and Strategies*. London: Sage.

Reid, G. (2003) *Dyslexia: A Practitioner's Handbook*. Chichester: Wiley.

Reid, G. and Green, S. (2007) *100 Ideas for Supporting Pupils with Dyslexia*. London: Continuum.

Renaldi, F. (2005) *Dyslexia and Design Technology*. London: David Fulton.

Tunmer, W. E. and Chapman, J. (1996) 'A developmental model of dyslexia. Can the construct be saved?' *Dyslexia*, 2:3, 179–89.

UBC Okanagan (2006) *A Guide for Effective Practices for Teaching Assistants Fall 2006*, available to download from http://web.ubc.ca/okanagan/ctl/ta/Teaching_Assistant_Manual.html, viewed 30 July 2007.